D1221042

Formerly Urban

New City Books

The New City Books series explores the intersection of architecture, landscape architecture, infrastructure, and planning in the redevelopment of the civic realm. Focusing on government sponsorship of design, the study of weak-market cities, contemporary American housing, and the role of a research university as a resource and collaborator, the series highlights the formative nature of innovative design and the necessity for strategies that trigger public and private support.

The New City Books series includes:

From the Ground Up
Innovative Green Homes

Formerly Urban
Projecting Rust Belt Futures

New Public Works
Architecture, Planning, and Politics

Modern American Housing
High-Rise, Reuse, Infill

American City "X"
Syracuse after the Master Plan

Formerly Urban

Projecting Rust Belt Futures

Edited by Julia Czerniak

With contributions by
McLain Clutter
Julia Czerniak
Don Mitchell
Edward Mitchell
Hunter Morrison
Marc Norman
Mark Robbins
David Grahame Shane
Roger Sherman
Charles Waldheim

Syracuse University
School of Architecture
and
Princeton Architectural Press

Published by
Princeton Architectural Press
37 East Seventh Street
New York, New York 10003
Visit our website at www.papress.com.

Syracuse University School of Architecture
Slocum Hall
Syracuse, New York 13244
www.soa.syr.edu

© 2013 Princeton Architectural Press

All rights reserved

Printed and bound in China

16 15 14 13 4 3 2 1 First edition

No part of this book may be used or
reproduced in any manner without written
permission from the publisher, except in the
context of reviews.

Every reasonable attempt has been made
to identify owners of copyright. Errors or
omissions will be corrected in subsequent
editions.

Series Editor: Mark Robbins
Design: Pentagram
Project Editor: Dan Simon

Special thanks to: Bree Anne Apperley,
Sara Bader, Janet Behning, Nicola Bednarek
Brower, Fannie Bushin, Megan Carey,
Carina Cha, Andrea Chlad, Benjamin English,
Russell Fernandez, Jan Haux, Diane Levinson,
Jennifer Lippert, Jacob Moore, Gina Morrow,
Katharine Myers, Margaret Rogalski, Elana
Schlenker, Sara Stemen, Andrew Stepanian,
Paul Wagner, and Joseph Weston of Princeton
Architectural Press —Kevin C. Lippert, publisher

The New City Books series is made possible
by a grant from the Rockefeller Foundation.
Additional funding is provided by the
Syracuse University School of Architecture,
Judith Greenberg Seinfeld, the National
Endowment for the Arts, The Richard H.
Driehaus Foundation, the Graham Foundation
for Advanced Studies in the Fine Arts, the
New York State Council for the Arts, Deutsche
Bank Americas Foundation, Furthermore: a
program of the J. M. Kaplan Fund, and the
Central New York Community Foundation.

Library of Congress
Cataloging-in-Publication Data

Formerly urban: projecting rust belt futures
/ edited by Julia Czerniak; with contributions
by McLain Clutter, Don Mitchell, Edward
Mitchell, Hunter Morrison, Marc Norman,
Mark Robbins, David Grahame Shane, Roger
Sherman, Charles Waldheim.

pages cm — (New city books)

Includes bibliographical references.

Papers presented at the Formerly Urban
conference, held Oct. 13–14, 2010, Syracuse
Unviersity, Syracuse, N.Y.

ISBN 978-1-61689-089-6 (hardcover:
alk. paper)
1. City planning—United States—Congresses.
2. Cities and towns—United States—
Congresses. 3. Deindustrialization—Social
aspects—United States—Congresses.
I. Czerniak, Julia, editor of compilation.
HT167.F677 2012
307.1'2160973—dc23

2012011927

Contents

Foreword
David Grahame Shane

The rapid urbanization of the North American continent is, from a global perspective, a remarkable achievement that inspired many other nations to follow a similar path. To Europeans in the nineteenth century, the speed of the process seemed extraordinary. The equally fast shift from cities based on agriculture and trading to a massive national industrial system made Chicago, Pittsburgh, Detroit, and New York City marvels of modernity that amazed Europeans and Asians alike. Many smaller cities like Cleveland, Ohio, and Buffalo, Rochester, and Syracuse, New York, rode this wave of industrial urbanization. Sadly, these cities failed to shift gears into the third phase of American urbanization, when industrial growth moved first to suburban locations, then to southern and western locations with many subsidies, and then out of the United States entirely into a global, corporate, networked economy.

This book sees hope in the multiple responses of various urban actors and strategies that acknowledge the narrative of industrial decline, ecological depredation, and human suffering presented at the "Formerly Urban" conference held at Syracuse University in 2010. The structure and organization of this conference looked forward to a fourth wave of American urbanization, one that deals with some of the negative consequences of the three earlier phases, traces of which litter the upstate landscape. Without nostalgia the speakers faced a tough future and found new possibilities for design and beauty in the desolate postindustrial landscape. The conference and now this volume serve important roles outlining a new approach to the art of building cities that is much more complex, subtle, remediated, mediated, and difficult than the previous simple narrative of endless physical and material progress. In making this much-needed revision, *Formerly Urban* points to a way that Americans can again link to the world by providing a more carbon-neutral path to a still dynamic, patch- and actor-driven urbanization.

Speed and the American Metropolis
The speed and scale of American modernity impressed the world in the nineteenth and early twentieth centuries. American industrialists learned from the chaotic and disorganized British Industrial Revolution

(described in detail by Eric Hobsbawm in *Industry and Empire,* 1968), scaling up the earlier model to meet a Continental demand. American corporations, after the Civil War, could operate across a continent. This allowed for massive economies of scale and developed the corporate capacity for complex organization, advertising, and marketing at a new vast scale in a single marketplace. Spectacular urban centers grew up in single generations, where the mechanized farming and railways of the Great Plains formed the basis for a rapid industrialization. These cities soon emerged to prominence as the grain-exporting capitals of the world, and their subsequent transformation into financial and cultural centers.

The development of the skyscraper, streetcar, and then railway suburbs followed, creating an image of the modern American metropolis that was spectacularly at odds with ancient metropolises such as Beijing. With its single center in the imperial Forbidden City, Beijing existed as a low-rise city for centuries as the seat of Chinese imperial power; it differed from European capitals like Berlin, Paris, and London, with their low-rise city silhouettes and grand military boulevards reserved for parades and bourgeois display. The Chicago Loop and New York's Wall Street shaped the modern metropolis into a capitalist emblem in the modern imagination, and the clusters of skyscrapers symbolized the rapid modernization of American society.

Industrial centers, like Pittsburgh and Detroit, mirrored this high-rise silhouette, as did smaller industrial cities like Buffalo, Cleveland, Rochester, and Syracuse, with their own clusters of pioneering skyscrapers and factories, housing and streetcar suburbs. These mini-metropolitan cities, based in industrialized, agricultural hinterlands and supported by coal, steam power, railways, and streetcars, produced a legacy of wealth and powerful civic actors. Even after the disappearance of the industry, these actors continued to control the institutions that created the modern city. The French philosopher Michel Foucault pointed to these instruments of modernity in his famous essay "Of Other Places." His list of institutions that created knowledge and power ranged from orphanages, hospitals, and courthouses to department stores, museums, libraries, and theaters.

The authors in this book provide plentiful evidence that many of these urban institutions are facing up to their responsibilities in difficult times and are seeking to create a new urban future no longer based on their industrial past. Big institutional organizations prove to be key civic

actors in this effort. They provide important stability after factories
have closed, neighborhoods have decayed, and populations have dwin-
dled. Foucault's laundry list proved accurate, as rectors of universities,
museum directors, and deans of medical and architecture schools have
stepped forward to help rescue their host cities across the American
Rust Belt.

Speed in the American Megalopolis

The rapid urbanization of America was followed by the equally rapid
invention of new urban forms for the automobile age of the late 1940s
and 1950s. As Donald Appleyard, Kevin Lynch, and John R. Myer
pointed out in *View from the Road* (1964), time, not distance, became
the important dimension, and the landscape, topography, and signage
became the markers of change. Architects Robert Venturi, Denise Scott
Brown, and Steven Izenour examined the design implications of the
new scale and speed associated with the automobile in *Learning from
Las Vegas* (1972), concentrating on the acres of parking lots, building
signage, and symbolic facades in a new "vast space."

Every American city and small town developed its equivalent of the
Vegas Strip as elements of the city moved with the millions of Americans
to the suburbs, creating a new urban form. Previously concentrated
urban services relocated to pavilions along shopping strips on "Miracle
Miles" just outside the municipal limits of their host cities, dodging
municipal taxes. In *Crabgrass Frontier: The Suburbanization of the United
States* (1987) urban historian Kenneth T. Jackson outlined the long historical background that led to the rise of the American suburban dream
and resulted, in the 1950s, in massive developments like the 4,400-acre
Levittown, Long Island. Jackson described how, over the course of fifteen
years, forty million people moved from American cities to suburbs.

The French geographer Jean Gottmann spelled out the consequences
of this new urban form in *Megalopolis: The Urbanized Northeastern
Seaboard of the United States* (1961), arguing that never had so many
people lived so well in a city without conflict. His megalopolis stretched
450 miles from Boston to Washington and contained thirty-two million
inhabitants, and he documented where the food, water, and energy
came from, as well as where the wastes went. When Gottmann wrote
Megalopolis, the interstate highway system was in its infancy, but infrastructure developed by the oil industry during World War II fueled a
new urban form with drive-in restaurants, cinemas, and gas stations.
At this time Detroit played an enormous role nationally, and then

internationally, as the home of the American auto industry. Its rise sponsored a wealthy suburban expansion. Planners like Constantinos Doxiadis began to think of Detroit on an enormous regional scale, arguing in his 1966 report for an inter-regional city that stretched all the way to Chicago.

Although the megalopolis drained population from the metropolis, it too was vulnerable, and eventually declined due to international oil price spikes, shifting consumer tastes, and marketing dynamics. With the high price of gasoline, the car no longer commands the road entirely as other users—bikes and pedestrians, even plants and retention ponds—are gaining space. Now there is an international trend to remove highways from downtowns and riverbeds; some of these projects are discussed in this book. Signage from strip malls and abandoned malls now evokes nostalgia, just as dead malls are topics of discussion for adaptive reuse by communities.

The Fragmentation of the American Metropolis

Three notable American authors reacted quickly to the dominant ideology of auto-based suburban expansion of the 1950s. In *The Death and Life of Great American Cities* (1961), Jane Jacobs (who had put a spike in Robert Moses's highway ambitions, helping to block his proposed LOMEX highway in lower Manhattan) sang the praises of the local community and the pedestrian "choreography" of the well-used, well-watched, small-scale street and sidewalk. Rachel Carson's *Silent Spring* (1962) announced the dangers of the petrochemical industry and its role in polluting land and water, endangering flora and fauna. The third author, Kevin Lynch, published *The Image of the City* (1960), which created a new language for mapping the inner city and for wayfinding. The book also showed the impact of the Boston Downtown Expressway on local Chinese, Italian, and other immigrant communities.

Architects like Welton Becket, John Graham, and Victor Gruen who worked for big department-store chains or mall developers advocated for shopping malls to be the new community centers of the megalopolis. Their plans created new urban fragments at suburban highway intersections. In *The Heart of Our Cities: The Urban Crisis: Diagnosis and Cure* (1964), Gruen described the developer's rule of thumb for the successful distribution of shopping malls in a multicentered, fragmented system: half a million people within a twenty- to thirty-minute driving radius with forty acres available for five thousand parking spaces. Gruen tried unsuccessfully to apply this formula to downtown

Rochester, where he developed a pioneering hybrid mall and tower scheme, the 1956 Rochester Square development. This project combined a suburban, interior mall on the dumbbell model with a mixed-use, pastel-colored office tower with a rooftop restaurant and bar. Gruen also pedestrianized Rochester's East Main Street, an experiment that did not last.

Lynch argued that malls were the only successful American urban designs, but he nonetheless worked with a team for the Boston Redevelopment Authority (BRA) to apply their logic to the city center. In 1959, his team led the BRA to focus its work on small, mall-like fragments downtown. As a result the BRA initiated a contextual zoning pattern that allowed for both a new civic center and the historic preservation of the Quincy Market, opening in 1976 as the first heavily subsidized "festival marketplace." Just as Disneyland had in its first year, this downtown mall attracted twelve million people.

Ten years before Rem Koolhaas published *Delirious New York: A Retroactive Manifesto for Manhattan* (1978), a similar concentration on urban fragments took place in New York City. Under the administration of Mayor John Lindsay the Urban Design Group emerged in the 1960s as a unit of the Planning Department. It used a strategy of fragmentation based on community interest and participation (learning from Jacobs) as well as incentives for developers and investors (learning from the BRA). When, in 1968, the City Council failed to pass the Planning Department's master plan, the Urban Design Group was able to develop a fragmentary Special Zoning District system and later Business Improvement Districts (BIDs). These later became staples of global urban design consultants and were exported to London, Hong Kong, Shenzhen, and even Moscow and St. Petersburg. "Special District" designations and tax-incentive schemes have also played a role in attempts to revive American Rust Belt cities, as discussed in this book.

Speed and American Megacities/Metacities
Toward the end of the twentieth century the speed of the transformations of the American city appeared to slow down. As Europe and Asia installed high-speed rail systems which made short-distance jet travel obsolete in urban corridors, America failed to make the same leap. At present the 118-mile train journey from New York to Albany takes 2 hours and 30 minutes, while the travel time for a comparable 108-mile journey in China, between Shanghai and Hangzhou, is 45 minutes. As European and Asian cities planned to shift from fossil fuel

dependence, following the Kyoto Accord, America again failed to move toward a green economy of solar cells, super-insulation, wind farms, and electric vehicles, ceding the lead position to Germany and Japan, and later to China.

As American investment in urban infrastructure slowed, American telecommunication corporations and media networks created a new kind of informational city or metacity. This city was different from the "global village" of instant communication that Marshall McLuhan, the media theorist, envisioned in *The Gutenberg Galaxy* (1961). McLuhan had imagined that satellite transmissions of news and entertainment via television would create a new global consciousness. Instead, mobile hand-held devices have created networks of personal communication—virtual urban villages—and reduced the importance of television networks (which had in turn reduced the importance of newspapers). The true power of these virtual urban villages manifests in the ability of diverse groups of individuals to coordinate actions in the city, ranging from flash mobs to political demonstrations.

The widespread distribution of personalized mass-communication systems has altered the transportation landscape. They allow just-in-time planning that makes slow trains less important. Train travel can become a time for working or watching a movie. Additionally, as described in this book, designers can now produce work anywhere in this network, musicians can distribute their music widely, or even create their own recording studios away from traditional media centers. Similarly, home offices can replace commuting to an office park, and home shopping on the internet substitutes for a journey to the mall.

In addition to the Rust Belt's newfound river valleys and water systems, some writers in this book comment on the region's desire for a new urban agricultural balance, sometimes described as a new rural-urban hybrid. In this system, landscape remediation is coupled with a drive for local food production. Small farmers have found a niche market that even supermarket chains cannot ignore. In Milwaukee, Sweet Water Organics operates an aquaponic fish and vegetable farm inside an old steel mill. It offers educational outreach to local schools and the surrounding neighborhood. The new modernity of the American city appears to include food production on an artisanal, Slow Food basis, breaking the cult of speed, just as light-speed communication systems traverse the countryside via fiber-optic cables and satellite.

Questions Raised by the Formerly Urban

What does "formerly urban" mean in the contemporary city when there are at least four competing urban models and many other variations? How does the observer define it? In the 1990s, for instance, Rem Koolhaas stood in the widely distributed American city—of malls and sprawling suburbs—and looked nostalgically at megaforms of the first American machine age like Rockefeller Center while he described European capitals as formerly urban, outdated slums. Making such a statement in the twenty-first century might be even more complicated, as there are multiple former urbanisms available, including Koolhaas's own widely distributed city with its megastructures positioned at intervals.

In an age of much uncertainty and strange recombinations of different polarities, we might ask exactly what "formerly" indicates in this context. Does it describe a collapsed system wherein a new realm of complexity and change is emerging? In specifically urban and architectural terms, what might be the consequences of these new amalgamations? This volume of essays begins to sketch out some valuable answers to these vexing questions. It shows new urban actors who operate in a confusing field where old categories, namely the communal directives of the command economy and the free-enterprise myths of American capitalism, no longer operate. The book points out what the symbolic intermediaries are: the icons, ideas, and myths that resonate in this newly diverse urban situation. It begins to spell out how citizens, communities, municipalities, legislators, institutions, and states might operate successfully in an impoverished America.

Preface and Acknowledgments

Formerly Urban: Projecting Rust Belt Futures is the second in the
New City Book series, published under the joint imprint of Princeton
Architectural Press and the Syracuse University School of Architecture.
Formerly Urban joins *From the Ground Up: Innovative Green Homes*
in examining issues pertaining to architecture, design, and urban
revitalization, in this case the future of regional shrinking cities.

The essays, commentary, and illustrative material contained in this
book were developed through a number of venues. One of these,
a two-day conference held at the Syracuse University School of
Architecture in October 2010, gathered twenty-one international
experts in architecture, landscape architecture, and urban design, as
well as planning, policy, finance, economics, and real estate development, to focus on the benefits of creating urbanity in weak-market
cities. Participants shared strategies for cities whose urban character
has devolved radically due to economic, demographic, and physical
change—cities that are now considered "formerly urban"—through
the lens of approaches to practice, shaping neighborhoods and regions,
the potentials of landscape, urbanity without density, and financing
design in weak markets. Many of the ideas and speculations that
resulted from this event were used to frame a conversation about
potential futures for the global phenomenon of cities that are growing
smaller. Prior to and following the conference, discussions and debates
about shrinking cities spawned numerous seminars and studios at the
School of Architecture, and brought the questions around its concerns
centrally to the school's pedagogy surrounding urbanism. All of this
interest and inquiry speaks to the relevance of this topic to the design
disciplines today.

Many organizations, institutions, and individuals have contributed to the making of this book. For providing support for the "Formerly Urban: Projecting Rust Belt Futures" conference, we are grateful to the Graham Foundation for Advanced Studies in the Fine Arts, the Central New York Community Foundation, and the Syracuse University School of Architecture. For enabling the realization of this book series, I sincerely thank the Rockefeller Foundation, whose mission to promote the well-being of humanity experiencing hardship and crisis resonates strongly with the challenges of individuals and communities in struggling Rust Belt cities. At Syracuse, I owe tremendous gratitude to University President and Chancellor Nancy Cantor for her vision and leadership regarding the remaking of our own "formerly urban" city in thoughtful and just ways, and to the School of Architecture's former dean, Mark Robbins, whose powerful drive moved us all forward toward meaningful work and emergent horizons. I would also like to acknowledge and thank Marilyn Higgins, vice president of community engagement and economic development, for advancing my under-standing of the crucial and creative role economics plays in realizing complex urban revitalization projects.

The presentations and commentary of the speakers and respondents at the conference stimulated our work. We thank Adriaan Geuze, McLain Clutter, Darren Petrucci, Mark Robbins, Anne Munly, Toni Griffin, Don Mitchell, Hunter Morrison, Damon Rich, Brian Lonsway, Jonathan Marvel, Edward Mitchell, Roger Sherman, Andrew Zago, Mark Linder, Eelco Hooftman, Sébastien Marot, Charles Waldheim, Theodore Brown, Marc Norman, Rosanne Haggerty, Mark Willis, and James Lima.

As teachers we are fortunate to engage with students who have helped us formulate our ideas over the last few years. Among them are students in Trevor Lee's and my Formerly Urban studio who helped to advance our thinking, including Chris DeRosa, Brandon Peterson, and Ming Gao; as well as students in my Cities Growing Smaller seminar, among them Hilary Barlow, Erwin Riefkohl, Nate Wooten, Timothy Gale, and particularly Nilus Klingel, who always had something smart to add to the discussion. Particular colleagues have contributed to our efforts in formulating strategies for working in formerly urban contexts; among them I would like to thank Charles Waldheim, Mark Robbins, James Lima, Terry Schwartz, Margaret Newman, Michael Bierut, Ted Brown, Mark Linder, and James Corner.

For their administrative assistance, I thank the School of Architecture administration and staff for their help in facilitating the conference: Randall Korman, Katryn Hansen, Mark Linder, Michelle Klock, Elaine Wackerow, Chuck Savage, and Andy Molloy. We acknowledge and thank those in architectural publishing who help us realize our projects, especially Mary Kate O'Brien, Clare Jacobson, Kate Norment, and Karen Stein.

I am indebted to the staff at UPSTATE: A Center for Design, Research, and Real Estate at the Syracuse University School of Architecture, for their tireless work and commitment. Joe Sisko, Jacob Brown, Trevor Lee, Nilus Klingel, and Mouzayan Al Kahlil were strong supporters. The conference and this book could not have happened without the rigorous work of UPSTATE: Research Fellow Peggy Tully, to whom I am indebted. As always, my efforts here owe tremendous gratitude to Mark, Azriel, and Lili, who enable me to pursue my interests.

Julia Czerniak
Director, UPSTATE: A Center for Design, Research, and Real Estate
Professor, Syracuse University School of Architecture

Introduction
Julia Czerniak

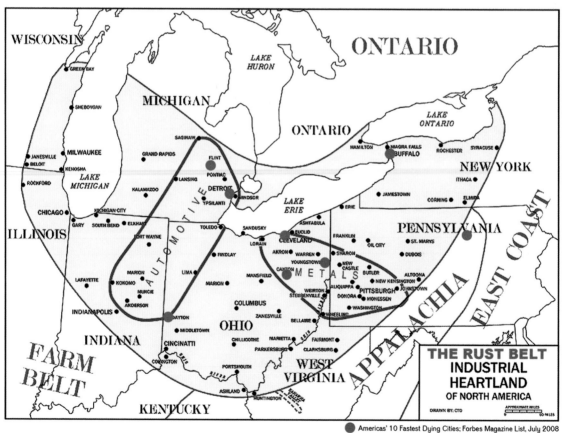

Americas' 10 Fastest Dying Cities; Forbes Magazine List, July 2008

The view of the Rust Belt from above at night is somewhat deceptive. Its shrinking cities coupled with its growing metropolises seem to blur into what urban critic Ed Soja calls "the post-metropolitan," a world that adds sixty million people to urban populations every year (fig. 1)[1]. But a striking statistic cited by the Berkeley Institute of Urban and Regional Development in 2005 tells another story: "Every 6th city in the world can be defined as a shrinking city."[2] Many of these, of course, are in the former industrial capitals of Western Europe and the eastern United States. Yet shrinkage is an international phenomenon, as cities are subject to today's space-altering, complex processes of deindustrialization, suburbanization, postsocialism, and globalization. It may surprise some, then, that Venice, Italy, where the tourist population reaches 1.5 times the city's population every day and 2,500 resident Venetians flee to the mainland every year; Hakodate, Japan, which has nearly doubled its land size with the acquisition of neighboring villages and towns while its density disperses; and Nilópolis, a municipality near Rio de Janeiro, Brazil, that has difficulty retaining its population in part because of its immense density, are all considered shrinking cities.[3] In other words, a label of "shrinking" can be based solely on a loss of resident population—not a loss of land area, density, jobs, or even urban life. A recent post to the website The Infrastructurist reminds us that cities listed as "shrinking" and "dying" are really just subject to "the bias and nature of our measures of progress and economic growth."[4] In other words, if cities are not considered to be growing by the traditional definitions, then they are considered to be dying.

Nonetheless, Rust Belt cities join other global cities in the challenges precipitated by population loss: the diminishment of social-welfare networks and basic services, the erosion of public school systems, the loss of industry, increasing amounts of tax delinquency and vacant land, and crumbling infrastructure that has a direct impact on public health, safety, and the environment. These cities also face less tangible but very real impacts on the quality of urban life.

To add to their already challenged status, Rust Belt cities were identified by *Forbes* in the summer of 2008 as seven of America's "10 fastest-dying cities" measured by "fleeing populations, painful waves of unemployment, and barely growing economies" (fig. 2).[5] Interestingly, these measures are based on figures for metropolitan areas, not just the cities themselves. Such areas typically exhibit a hollowing core but a growing periphery. The *Forbes* report showed

Opposite, top: Fig. 1. North America at night showing large urban agglomerations

Opposite, bottom: Fig. 2. The Rust Belt, formerly America's heartland, with "fastest-dying cities" marked in red

that between 2000 and 2008 the metropolitan area of Youngstown, Ohio, lost 32,000 people, Buffalo 42,000, and Cleveland a staggering 51,000 people.[6] Later in 2008, of course, massive failures of financial institutions in the United States subjected these struggling cities to new pressures of foreclosure.[7]

Effects of the financial crisis put the apparently tired topic of shrinking cities in alarming need of new attention as other American cities, especially in the Sunbelt, began to face the challenges surrounding depopulation. Notwithstanding provocative work to date, design-driven change in these cities has been slow and must be revisited. Such cities present a challenging design context that is compounded by their degree of dependence on public funding, a lack of professional design expertise, and a resistance to change.

Formerly Urban

The phrase "formerly urban" is, admittedly, not of our own creation. It has been used by architect and urbanist Rem Koolhaas to describe the urban context of Houston, Texas, where he calls for "a less substantial, less oppressive, and less vulnerable condition that offers the benefit of the urban condition."[8] The collection of essays in this book helps us to imagine that scenario.

"Formerly urban" is both a description, then, and a provocation. Is being formerly urban tantamount to giving up on the urban, as many who react to the phrase believe it suggests? Is the phrase productive, as urban designer Roger Sherman suggests in his essay here, only when it is considered a symptom rather than a condition? Is its import greatest when it does not exclusively refer to a context of loss? Or does "formerly urban" simply prompt us to conceptually expand what we mean by the urban and test our ability to innovate? These questions suggest that the city, the metropolis, and urbanity are all at stake here. The authors included in this volume believe that a shrinking city—despite its loss of population and its challenged state—is not necessarily dying but is often in need of new strategies to activate urban life.

Yet the subject of the formerly urban territory of the Rust Belt preoccupies more than just those in the design and planning fields; it is of interest to almost every discipline and profession today—from film to politics to journalism. All of this work shapes our culture's expanding perception of the region.

Contemporary film and television use the shrinking Rust Belt cities of Flint and Detroit, Michigan; Cleveland, Youngstown, and Dayton, Ohio; Buffalo and Syracuse, New York; and Scranton, Pennsylvania, as subjects and settings. Perpetuating the negative, Buffalo appears as a gray and dismal city in the opening scenes of Vincent Gallo's *Buffalo 66,* into which the main character is released from prison. Scranton gets somewhat better treatment in NBC's TV series *The Office.* Interestingly, the program has provided the city with a micro economy of tourism; the Scranton Chamber of Commerce even offers a map to guide visitors to locations central to the show. Detroit receives a lot of media attention. Clint Eastwood's *Gran Torino* pictures a changing Detroit neighborhood controlled by gangs and violence. The city is treated as a character in ABC's homicide detective show *Detroit 1-8-7.* The number, the producers of the show explain, is street slang for murder and highlights the fact that this smaller big city is a perennial contender for murder capital of the United States. VBS.TV recently produced a three-part video sequence called *Detroit Lives* to counter, they explain, the negative media coverage of the city. *Time* magazine focused on the city in a yearlong project called "Assignment Detroit." Though the magazine's October/November 2009 cover announced "The Tragedy of Detroit," the articles within described small steps the Motor City was taking toward its rejuvenation.[9]

The formerly urban territory of the Rust Belt also preoccupies our real capital through the efforts of politicians. Pittsburgh hosted the G-20 economic summit in 2009, where President Obama plugged the city as the type of place by which to measure our nation's future prosperity. Pittsburgh's mayor, Luke Ravenstahl, added that "now Pittsburgh has a chance to exchange its pervasive imagery as a gritty, dying Rust Belt city" with a "green" image based on its new economy—biotechnology and clean energy.[10] Both the media and politicians suggest that the issues these cities face extend "from the crisis of manufacturing to the challenges of urban planning."[11]

It is no surprise that planning, a discipline close to architecture, land-scape architecture, and design, is invoked, for these disciplines have been preoccupied with the Rust Belt for quite some time. Most compre-hensively, the two volumes produced by the "Shrinking Cities" project (2005 and 2006, respectively) present research about and strategies for shrinking cities globally.[12] The project catalogs urban operations and a host of projects that deconstruct (demolish or contract), reorganize (through self-organization or entrepreneurship), and imagine (through

RUST BELT
FORMERLY AMERICA'S
INDUSTRIAL HEARTLAND

WEAK MARKET CITIES:
"Core cities that were once the economic, social and
cultural hubs of their regions, but are now looking to
find a new economic niche." Anne Power

UPSTATE: A Center for Design, Research, and Real
Estate.   Source: The Brookings Institution

Fig. 3. Weak-market cities
in the United States

marketing and branding) the shrinking city.[13] Additionally, *Stalking Detroit* (2001) was one of the first publications to foreground scenarios for vacant properties in that city by choreographing the process of "decommissioning, depopulating, and reconceiving" their use not just as land, but as hybridized landscape and social space.[14]

Many organizations target planners as their audience. The Shrinking Cities Institute at the Cleveland Urban Design Collaborative recognizes the need to envision a future for some cities that is "smaller and smarter, rather than bigger and better" and to explore the idea of planned shrinkage that includes the now familiar strategies of demolishing underutilized housing, removing redundant streets, and downsizing municipal infrastructure to correspond to declining population. The institute renames the "shrinking city" a "city growing smaller," a twist of language that casts these places in a more positive light. The Shrinking Cities Research Group within Berkeley's Center for Global Metropolitan Studies is a recognized leader for its case-study research on the role that different policies and strategies have in the regeneration of shrinking cities, regions, and suburbs.

Projecting Futures

Projecting positive futures for Rust Belt cities suggests that many
people see something other than decline and disinvestment in the
formerly urban city. They see an opportunity to provide the benefits
of urbanity in weak-market cities, cities that Anne Powers of the
London School of Economics says have "lost their former rationale and
are looking for new economic niches."[15] Although this projection is
grounded in the Rust Belt, its value extends beyond it, as many of the
shrinking cities discussed here can be generalized to serve as laborato-
ries for other weak-market cities across the United States, such as
Los Angeles, Miami, and Philadelphia (fig. 3).

Formerly Urban: Projecting Rust Belt Futures draws on the knowledge
of experts in architecture, landscape architecture, and urban design—
as well as planning, policy, finance, economics, and real estate development—to project brighter futures for America's Rust Belt through
their research and practice and to advance speculation about remaking
its shrinking cities. These experts recognize that activating urban life
requires developing strategies that are asset-based and economical,
reconsidering ways that urbanity is produced (from historical notions
of density to more contemporary programming strategies), and imagining a new kind of city full of promise and potential.

The essays collected here variously examine ways in which formerly
urban cities can produce vibrant urban life in the context of diffuse
urban fabrics; explore strategies of advocacy and education, shrinkage,
consolidation, and land banking; revisit the potentials of landscape
urbanism to imagine, catalyze, build upon, and maintain vast amounts
of emerging land; speculate on the expanded ecological and civic roles
that infrastructure can play in the city; and probe financing structures
for innovative development in weak-market cities.

The Essays

Reimagining this altered terrain calls for design practices that engage the
economic, ecological, social, and political aspects of cities. The essays
collected here are reflections by leading architects, landscape architects,
planners, and experts in the field of affordable housing development and
finance who recognize that projective work in these challenged contexts
lies at the intersection of design, policy, and finance.

Although the design practices for Rust Belt cities draw on speculation
both within and outside of the Rust Belt region, contributors

Mark Robbins and McLain Clutter work close to home in the regional hot spots of Syracuse and Cleveland, respectively. In his opening essay, "It's (Not) Just the Money," Mark Robbins—architect, artist, and former dean of Syracuse University's School of Architecture—focuses on ways to coalesce capital, expertise, and political will to remake the physical form of the American city. He argues that a creative team of professionals is needed to navigate the intersections between commerce and the public good. Using examples of architecture, landscape architecture, and planning in the typical shrinking city of Syracuse, he describes innovations that were made possible only through the vision and commitment of the city's multiple public and private partners. Observing that there is typically no legislated voice for design as an essential component of the development process, Robbins advances ways to accomplish multiple goals with a single investment. He argues for a compelling working model that combines academic, economic, social, environmental, and urbanistic concerns with design excellence.

In "Cleveland: Medi-Plex City," Clutter probes the economic, intellectual, and aesthetic roots of the Cleveland Clinic's symbiosis with Cleveland—once the fourth-largest city in the United States. The clinic, the city's medical namesake, is now Cleveland's largest employer and the cornerstone of its economy. Over the past twenty years, the clinic has developed acres of the city's East Side while developing a symbiotic relationship with Cleveland's urban blight (fig. 4). Clutter posits a framework for designers to rethink the relationship between Cleveland and its clinic, urging the emergence of a new type at the synthesis of urbanism and urban hospital—a strategy useful for all cities with strong medical economies.

In their respective essays in this book, planner Hunter Morrison and geographer Don Mitchell discuss seemingly antithetical tactics for re-creating just and healthy urban neighborhoods. In "Lessons Learned from a Shrinking City: Youngstown 2010 and Beyond," Morrison focuses on a shrinking city that has received national and international attention as one of the first American cities to acknowledge, as a matter of public policy, the goal of being a smaller but more sustainable city. As a result of taking this bold stand, Youngstown has become known as an innovator in redefining the future of America's historically industrial cities, known variously, Morrison suggests, as "shrinking cities," "forgotten cities," "weak-market cities," and "cities in transition." Morrison argues that these cities have only recently become the topic of national policy debate, despite the fact that the forces of systematic disinvestment

and global industrial restructuring have been in play for several decades. As one of the leaders of the award-winning Youngstown 2010 Plan, Morrison discusses the planning process and the community's accomplishments—and disappointments—since the city adopted this vision in 2005 (fig. 5). He discusses the lessons he has learned from his experience in Youngstown and the implications of the city's pioneering path for other similarly situated American communities.

In "Retrenchment, Revitalization, or the Right to the City?: Four Theses," Mitchell raises the question of political orientation— a question that, he argues, has to be at the root of any progressive

Fig. 4. Cleveland, Ohio

Fig. 5. Youngstown, Ohio

Fig. 6. Picture the Homeless

attempt to create just urban neighborhoods in the wake of two generations of active disinvestment. Arguments in favor of retrenchment—
or shrinking the city—hold both environmental and social appeal, but
Mitchell builds the case that if we are serious about making our cities
for the people who live in them, we need to reorient our interventions.
Under the banner of "the right to the city," Mitchell suggests and
describes ways in which our thinking about struggling neighborhoods
should be oriented toward not just remaking the city but also participating in its remaking. In this way, he argues, a more fully vibrant
urban life might prevail (fig. 6).

In their essays, urban designer Roger Sherman and architect Edward
Mitchell reassess the promises and purposes of urban design. Both
speculate on how the traditional mechanisms of the discipline are being
replaced by the notion that the effects and benefits of the "urban" can
be produced by alternative means. In this way they join the radical
reassessment under way for at least two decades of the promise
and purpose of urban design made through the famous critiques of
modernism—by Jane Jacobs, Kevin Lynch, Aldo Rossi, Colin Rowe,
Rem Koolhaas, and Robert Venturi and Denise Scott Brown—which
now seem inadequate.[16] Urban agents, among them architects, planners, policy makers, developers, and engineers, are challenging
fundamental assumptions about density, programmatic diversity,
formal and spatial organization, scale, and infrastructure. This is no
less true in shrinking cities like Syracuse than in hypertrophic centers
in the developing world. Fewer people and more open space—the loss
of density—do not preclude the possibility of active urban life, but
designing for this condition requires new strategies.

In "Strange Attractors: The Catalytic Agency of Form," Sherman explores how the central problem of urbanism no longer concerns manipulating and distributing physical density—he cites Los Angeles as a growing city that still has only 25 percent of its land occupied by buildings—but rather parsing and managing the unprecedented density of information about a city toward its future transformation. He argues that what postsuburban models of urbanization may lack in literal density is ironically made up for (through technologies such as GPS sensing and GIS) by the ever-growing density of information about its habits, dynamics, stakeholders, and property values. Exploring the value of geo-data as a means by which to identify, represent, and ultimately attract the complex overlap of urban audiences and subcultures, he explores a largely untapped opportunity for architecture to recover its urban agency. Specifically, he advances design strategies that put forth new forms of urbanity through the exploration of more varied, if provisional, zones of collective life—what he has provocatively referred to as hot spots in an otherwise cool residual field.

In his essay "Pits and Piles in the Non-Concept City: Luzerne County, Pennsylvania," Mitchell speculates on strategies for what he calls articulating intensity in attenuated spatial fields and filling voids that are the necessary symbiotic by-product of capital. He argues that an urbanism without density would require a public expression that is blank and projective but maintains the incongruous and entropic nature of the site—both pit and pile, abstract and still, saturated and volatile, an infinite void that is a multitude of holes. Using his own work with the Earth Conservancy, he addresses these theoretical assertions through practical necessities located in transportation, water management, energy, and programming to revitalize an abandoned coal mine in the Luzerne Valley. Strategies for over 16,000 acres of properties include several distinct political communities and move from regional planning to detailed investigations, including tapping a one-hundred-year-old mine fire.

Probably no other discipline is so called to arms to assist in projecting futures for the Rust Belt city as landscape, given the abundance of vacant or underutilized land that has emerged in deindustrialized cities. This land's future use is complicated by challenges related to population loss, environmental degradation, and profoundly inadequate resources to both build and maintain projects. In both my own essay and that by Charles Waldheim, we engage the landscape discipline in ways that foreground not only how it performs, the agenda of which is most advanced by landscape urbanism, but also how it appears, its often dismissed but inescapable counterpart.

The intent of my own text, "Landscape's M.O.," is to share my perceptions and conceptions of urban landscape's appearance and performance in four shrinking Rust Belt cities experienced during a thousand-mile drive from Syracuse to Detroit and back again. My perception of these cities was previously formed through maps, images, or short visits, and my knowledge of them through projects and media. Using photographs and drawings, I aimed to record how landscape in such places operates when left to its own logic—that is, how landscape looks and behaves when it is not constrained by maintenance and management, muscled instead by ecological, socioeconomic, and political forces. My views on the ground formed the basis of a set of possibilities for these and other formerly urban cities (fig. 7)

In "Detroit, *Disabitato*, and the Origins of Landscape," Waldheim—who is best known for his advocacy of landscape as *the* discipline to address the making of the contemporary city—discusses the disciplinary realignments that inevitably result from addressing, or are even required to address, the environments left behind after urban disinvestment and decay. Drawing parallels between Detroit today and ancient Rome, Waldheim reveals that the very origins of landscape have equally been informed by and are historically bound up with the depopulation, abandonment, and decay of previously urbanized territories (fig. 8). In this way he suggests that the formerly urban indeed has a long history, and in so doing presupposes that a close reading of landscape's past is a prerequisite for projecting its engagement with future work.

In this book's final essay, Marc Norman, vice president of Deutsche Bank America's Community Development Finance Group, explains that those advocating for innovative design in Rust Belt cities must confront the realities of working in weak markets. In these cities, municipalities generally find themselves with unmanageable vacant property, aging infrastructure, degraded environmental conditions, and exacerbated social inequities. They lack the resources to confront these problems due to a long-shrinking population and the resulting depleted tax base. These cities, often in dire need of new directions for public services, infrastructure, and economic development, tend to have the least capacity to foster and encourage innovation. And yet they have many resources to leverage, such as good housing stock and historically significant academic institutions. Exploring the relationship between

innovative design and "value creation" challenges developers, policy-makers, and designers to turn crisis into opportunity.[17]

Fig. 7. Flint, Michigan

Fig. 8. Detroit, Michigan

Toward this end, Norman's essay, "Underwriting Icicles and Leveraging Sidewalks," looks at specific financing structures that create new ways to unlock the value of buildings and neighborhoods in weak markets. Arguing that with standard bank underwriting methodologies predicated on loan-to-value and future property appreciation, older urban neighborhoods are often locked out of conventional debt markets and trapped in an ever-downward spiral of deterioration and accelerating capital outflows. He proposes that through energy retrofits, efficiency upgrades, and transit-oriented development, new methodologies for underwriting and innovative leveraging mechanisms are being developed to create value and produce revitalized, healthy communities. The potential relationship between design experimentation, finance mechanisms, and policy innovation is without a doubt the most fertile territory in which to work for projecting Rust Belt futures.

Our efforts in this collection are grounded in the belief that design—and its interface with multiple disciplines and professions—plays a central role in the revitalization of shrinking cities. Designers should seize, or in some instances produce, the opportunity to be the link among multiple institutional frameworks—the university, the government, the development community, and private foundations—to implement innovative design. Designers must also participate at the inception of specific projects within this complex network, helping to shape both urban design policy and the design of public works. These essays begin to suggest the way.

1   Edward Soja, "Exopolis: The Restructuring of Urban Form," in *Postmetropolis:
     Critical Studies of Cities and Regions* (Oxford: Blackwell Publishers, 2000), 233–63.

2   See Berkeley Shrinking Cities Group (2005), http://www.ced.berkeley.edu/research
     institutes.

3   For more information on these cities, see The Shrinking Cities Project,
     http://www.shrinkingcities.com.

4   Posted by Peter Kageyama, author of *For the Love of Cities,* on The Infrastructurist,
     http://www.infrastructurist.com, June 13, 2011.

5   Joshua Zumbrun, "America's Fastest-Dying Cities," Forbes.com, August 5, 2008.

6   Ibid.

7   For more on the parallels between the Rust Belt and the Sunbelt, see Justin B. Hollander's
     *Sunburnt Cities: The Great Recession, Depopulation and Urban Planning in the American
     Sunbelt* (New York: Routledge, 2011).

8   Rem Koolhaas, "LITE CITY," in Rem Koolhaas and Bruce Mau, eds., *S,M,L,XL* (New York:
     Monacelli Press, 1998), 904. The full citation reads, "It is clear on any drive through
     Houston that what is needed is a science of desettlement—an art of erasure—the
     development of 'occupying' formerly urban territory (park is not by any stretch of the
     imagination the right word) but with a less substantial, therefore less oppressive and
     less vulnerable kind of urban condition—catalytic chains and patterns of unpredictable
     events—without the weight of matter—call it Lite City."

9   See Daniel Okrent's cover story, "The Tragedy of Detroit," *Time*, October 5, 2005.

10   Ian Urbina, "For Pittsburgh, G-20 Meeting Is a Mixed Blessing," *New York Times*,
     September 23, 2009.

11   See John Huey, "Assignment Detroit: Why Time Inc. Is in Motown,"
     http://www.time.com/time/magazine/article/0,9171,1926008.html, September 24, 2009.

12   *Shrinking Cities: Volume 1, International Research* and *Volume 2, Interventions*,
     ed. Philipp Oswalt et al. (Ostfildern-Ruit: Hatje Cantz, 2005 and 2006).

13   Ibid., vol. 1.

14   Of particular interest is Charles Waldheim and Marili Sanots-Munné's essay
     "Decamping Detroit," from which this excerpt is taken. See *Stalking Detroit*
     (Barcelona: Actar, 2001), 104–21.

15   The complete citation is: "We define 'weak market cities' as core cities that were once the
     economic, social and cultural hubs of their regions. They matured during the industrial era,
     when spatial attributes were key; since the end of World War II and the transition to the
     post-industrial era, however, they have lost their former rationale and are looking to find
     a new economic niche." See http://sticerd.lse.ac.uk/case/_new/research/weakmarketcities/
     default.asp

16   Thanks to Mark Linder for his help in formulating the original "Formerly Urban:
     Projecting Rust Belt Futures" conference session topic, "Urbanity without Density."

17   Thanks to James Lima, partner in HR&A Advisors, Inc., for the strong direction he provided
     for the conference session topic "Innovating Design in Weak Markets."

It's Not (Just) the Money

Mark Robbins

Previous page: Fig. 1.
The Warehouse, Syracuse,
New York, Gluckman Mayner
Architects, 2005

In the fall of 2010, as an $814 billion stimulus package was nearing exhaustion, President Obama proposed an additional $50 billion transportation program. Promoted as necessary to strengthen the economy and create jobs, it was estimated to meet just one quarter of the need for transportation infrastructure repair. Yet the proposal was an important action, not only because it included the creation of a National Infrastructure Bank, but because, according to news reports, the administration believed it would "bolster political support as a White House priority."[1] No new projects were discussed and total funding for the six-year package was not decided, but the spending plan tied infrastructure and the physical environment to economic futures as part of a public effort to galvanize lawmakers.

Investment in infrastructure is only a part of the larger task of rebuilding American cities. The allocation of public funds is critical, but their best use requires a coordinated engagement of expertise and advocacy for progressive work. The success of these ventures depends on a vision that includes architecture, engineering, design, and planning as well as effective civic leadership. Getting capital, expertise, and political will to coincide is no small feat, and the ability to discern the impact of physical planning and to evaluate alternatives needs to be paired with a compelling translation at a public level.

Within this matrix, especially in the postindustrial American city, nonprofit institutions—such as universities and hospitals—have increasingly engaged with governmental entities as partners in redevelopment. Reductions in manpower and professional expertise in municipal government have increased the potential importance of this role. Beyond financial investment, academic institutions can encourage a longer view by stimulating research and cultivating new models, leveraging implementation, and providing broad intellectual programming. Each sector—market, academy, and government—is changed by the interaction, which influences the quality of the decisions that are made.

This essay focuses on the intersection that is required among institutions to remake the physical form of the American city, citing examples of architecture, landscape architecture, and planning. It describes in greater detail the broad range of work implemented in recent years in the city of Syracuse, New York, through the leadership of Syracuse University, its School of Architecture, and its multiple public and private partners.

Fig. 2. Frank R. Lautenberg Rail Station, Secaucus, New Jersey, Brennan Beer Gorman/Architects (architect of record), 2003

The projects described in this essay are civic in nature. They innovatively respond to current conditions, investing in ways that the marketplace cannot or does not afford, in order to project more complex, responsive futures. This type of work risks experimentation and thus adds to the fund of disciplinary research. It offers examples of what is possible while increasing urban activity and density, which has an important practical and symbolic role. As the resulting value of a city and its assets is reaffirmed, morale and the economy improve. The sponsoring institutions benefit from creating a more desirable urban context, but the aspirations and outcome of this work have greater civic and academic worth.

Government Spending

During the economic prosperity of the 1990s, governments in Europe, Asia, and Latin America demonstrated inventive solutions for transit, infrastructure, and residential planning. Santiago Calatrava's structurally expressive Oriente Station in Lisbon, Norman Foster's Beijing Airport, and West 8's docklands redevelopment in Amsterdam are often cited in this regard. By contrast, in the United States a project like the 2003 Allied Junction/Secaucus Transfer Station (also known as the Frank R. Lautenberg Rail Station) offers a counterexample (fig. 2). Beyond its sheer physical gracelessness, the structure is striking for the time and expense it took to build, as well as for the myriad ways in which it has failed to perform. Rising above the gray horizon of the New Jersey Turnpike, the $1.25 billion project, which was in development for thirty years, was heralded as "revolutionary" when it was finally completed. Conceived as a public-private partnership, the station was to have 3.5 million square feet for office space, a hotel, a conference center, and retail outlets—none of which have been built. The station was meant to serve seventy thousand people per day, but currently serves an estimated eight thousand. Projects like this can reinforce skepticism about public-private partnerships among lawmakers and the public.

At various points in U.S. history, however, public works were the focus of both investment and innovation. From L'Enfant's plan for Washington, D.C., to the Hoover Dam and Cape Canaveral, their importance was symbolic and practical, representing civic will and function. Their design acted as the nexus between social, economic, and political spheres. A few notable examples continue at the federal level of processes that demonstrate the value of design, such as the Design Excellence Program of the General Services Administration and the Mayors' Institute on City Design of the National Endowment for the Arts (NEA).

Entities like these suggest expertise that is missing in the majority of municipalities in the United States that do not have professional design staff and so outsource decision-making, ceding much of the development process to commercial interests. This can yield a condition within the built environment akin to what social scientists refer to as the "hollow state," in which the bureaucracy functions but there are no longer internal experts to make decisions based on content and value. The diminishment of the state's role in decisions about the public good finds a parallel in the design of cities, infrastructure, and public buildings.

Good Work Needs Multiple Alignments

The popular and transformative Olympic Sculpture Park in Seattle was completed in 2007 at a cost of roughly $62 million. The park has won numerous awards and is one of the strongest examples in the nation of progressive work on the urban scale. Designed by Weiss/Manfredi Architecture/Landscape/Urbanism, the project reclaimed a 9-acre brownfield site in one of the last remaining downtown waterfront development areas. Mimi Gardner Gates, director of the Seattle Art Museum, initiated the idea of an outdoor sculpture park, and through collaboration with the Trust for Public Land assembled the private property and public rights-of-way. Olympic Sculpture Park received $20 million for an operating endowment from Jon and Mary Shirley. (Jon Shirley was the museum's board chairman and former COO of Microsoft.) In 2000 the project received a modest grant from

New Public Works—a pilot program sponsored by the NEA to fund public design competitions—that assisted with the selection process and provided a federal imprimatur. Given the hybrid nature of the park (architecture, art, landscape, and infrastructure all played a role in its design), a bold selection process was needed. The weight of the competition and a strong design animated public and private interests.

Olympic Sculpture Park represents an effective combination of philanthropy and public moneys with the political will of committed public servants. It required an institution with the vision to hire gifted architects, who were inventive and resilient enough for the rigors of public work. The project recalls an earlier era of less-mobile corporate wealth, when enlightened companies invested in their cities. Museums, as well as universities and hospitals, can now assume this larger civic role.

Twenty years ago in San Jose, California, it was the commitment of the mayor's office that helped transform a 3-mile length on the river's edge into Guadalupe River Park. The design succeeds in restructuring the relationship of the river with the city of San Jose. Designed over a ten-year period by Hargreaves Associates, it comprises a flood-control project integrated with a park. On the advice of the city architect, the city hired Hargreaves and their design team in an effort to provide an alternative to the original U.S. Army Corps of Engineers (USACE) scheme. Hargreaves was empowered to hire engineers, and through extensive laboratory modeling was able to prove that this proposal could perform better than the earlier scheme proposed by the USACE. The firm assembled a team of scientists—including a hydrologist, a geomorphologist, and a specialist in habitat restoration—and completed the park in 1999 at a cost of $60 million.

Mary Margaret Jones, the principal-in-charge for the project, has suggested in an interview about public work that its success stemmed from an approach that did not draw an artificial separation between infrastructure and design, between science and art. Understanding the science—for example, the patterns of silt deposition and water flow were extensively tested—was essential to make a convincing case across bureaucratic channels for a rigorous synthetic response. Hargreaves Associates has since worked on a variety of waterfront projects in Chattanooga, Nashville, Knoxville, and Richmond.

The University as Client and Resource
With few exceptions, the modern American city has not been a world

model in providing innovative housing, transportation, schools, or public landscapes. As much as such efforts depend on funding, they also require technical expertise, political will, and public support. A project's success can often be traced to a champion who understands the long-term value of good inventive work and who has the ability to convey this value effectively. The specific agent might be from the realm of philanthropy, government, or local civic, cultural, or educational institutions.

With cuts to the federal budget for community redevelopment, the nation's poorest neighborhoods will no doubt face the cancellation of projects and fewer new proposals. Central New York is a good example of a region in which need outstrips available funds, and it is instructive how choices are made for the use of these limited funds. Congressman James Walsh secured more than $900 million in federal funds earmarked for Central New York during his twenty years in Congress.[2] Another $10 million annually went to the city of Syracuse for community development over the same period, according to estimates of the Department of Neighborhood and Business Development.[3] And, according to Commissioner Paul Driscoll, "the city was completely unprepared to expend these funds when they first arrived. No plans, no design standards, no real way for the public to weigh in on these investment decisions." Even given the immense expense of capital work, this level of investment at the scale of a city of 145,000 people has the potential for a concentrated impact and a consistent citywide approach to planning and public works. The issue is both the insufficiency of funds and their deployment and the need for increasingly opportunistic projects.[4]

Universities in urban settings have the potential to spearhead more innovative, long-range goals and processes than local political cycles encourage. They increasingly provide both intellectual and financial capital for projects outside their traditional bounds. This is especially true in municipalities within the Rust Belt, in which the lack of resources and expertise within the public sector is often greatest. Crossing between for-profit and not-for-profit entities, the university can provide a nucleus around which activities in multiple disciplines can occur—a cross section of the economic and social welfare of a region.

Where government has increasingly withdrawn from making or revising propositions about the public realm, the university can galvanize disparate entities for projective work. Under the leadership of Chancellor Nancy Cantor, Syracuse University has led projects—ranging across a variety of sectors, including education, the arts, economic development, and urban development—that have begun to have a visible impact. The development of multiple consortia offers a model for interaction that is asset-based and understands local resources to include campus, city, and region. Within this milieu, the Syracuse University School of Architecture operates critically within the city as a place for curricular as well as professional engagement.

The chancellor created the position of university senior advisor for architecture and urban initiatives, which I held as the dean of the School of Architecture, to foster progressive design strategies both on and off campus. Working with the director of campus planning, design, and construction and multiple other stakeholders on selecting the architects and landscape architects for various projects has set the stage for innovative design. The conspicuous support of the university's senior officer for the new position publicly highlighted the role of design within the university.

The university's first major foray off campus in recent history was the 2005 renovation of a 140,000-square-foot warehouse building in downtown Syracuse for the temporary home of the Syracuse University School of Architecture, designed by Gluckman Mayner Architects. Though the university could have leased office space at an off-campus site for the school, this would have incurred an annual cost and would have no collateral positive impact (fig. 1).[5] Because of this new building, students now work in the city and an underutilized property has an active hybrid use. While the Warehouse project faced the challenges of schedule, financing, and approvals of institutional work, the parameters were more discrete than, for instance, undertaking the Connective Corridor—a large-scale infrastructure project shepherded by the university whose route links campus with downtown and the Near Westside neighborhood (fig. 3). The mix of public and private landownership, local and state jurisdiction, and varied sources of funding for the corridor make for greater complexity in its implementation—a parallel to the challenges of procuring professional design services across various regulatory bodies. Here again the establishment of a new position of vice president for community engagement and economic development to coordinate this work marked the recognition of the potential of design in urban revitalization and the role of the university in supporting innovation.

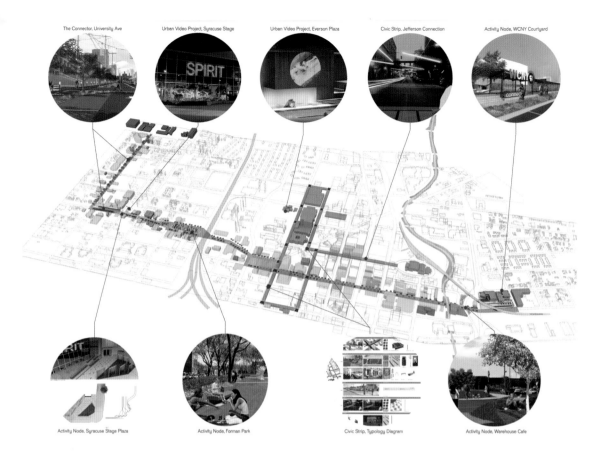

The Connector, University Ave

Urban Video Project, Syracuse Stage

Urban Video Project, Everson Plaza

Civic Strip, Jefferson Connection

Activity Node, WCNY Courtyard

Activity Node, Syracuse Stage Plaza

Activity Node, Forman Park

Civic Strip, Typology Diagram

Activity Node, Warehouse Cafe

Fig. 3. The Connective Corridor, Syracuse, New York, 2006–present, showing route, nodes, and cultural institutions

Each building project can perform broadly to benefit a neighborhood and extend the impact of the investment beyond a single structure. For instance, a new on-campus residence hall was designed with a glass-enclosed cafeteria at ground level and forms a courtyard with an earlier 1960s dormitory slab, creating a recreational space and activating the street (fig. 4). The off-campus Warehouse renovation responded to an immediate need for swing space, and the university's decision to use a building downtown and to purchase rather than lease created a permanent interdisciplinary arts and design center as a hub. It established an anchor at the edge of a pedestrian-oriented district adjacent to other arts-related facilities and has spurred private real estate acquisition and development—a textbook redevelopment strategy. Accomplishing multiple goals with a single investment, especially in challenging economic circumstances, serves as a compelling model. Academic, economic, social, environmental, and urbanistic concerns coincide with excellent design.

Informed Change

UPSTATE: A Center for Design, Research, and Real Estate in the Syracuse University School of Architecture bridges academic and professional work and serves as the transfer point for information through programming that is curricular as well as public. Since its inception in 2005, UPSTATE: has grown as a resource for the university, the city of Syracuse, and other cities beyond the region. It is led by professor Julia Czerniak, who with a staff of architects and landscape architects pursues research through studio-based projects and provides design expertise for built work, such as the Connective Corridor and work on the city's Near Westside. National design competitions, exhibitions, and symposia have assayed the city of Syracuse at a number of levels, bringing its mayor, chancellor, and leading design professionals together with students and faculty, as well as audiences of practitioners and residents (fig. 5). The presence of the center enhances disciplinary skills for students and faculty while providing wider exposure to strategies for planning, real estate development, landscape architecture, and architecture.

Fig. 4. Ernie Davis Residence Hall, Syracuse University, Mack Scogin Merrill Elam Architects, 2010

Fig. 5. UPSTATE: programming, 2005–10, Syracuse University School of Architecture. "UPSTATE: Downtown" brought the Syracuse University chancellor and the mayor of Syracuse together with noted architects, planners, and landscape architects in the context of a discussion of design and urban revitalization with students and faculty. "UPSTATE: Public-Private" focused on real estate development in weak-market cities and was paired with the exhibition "Syracuse Builds," which documented projects for the city. "Writing the City" and "Formerly Urban" presented urban design research and framed propositions for urban growth at the national and international level. The results of series of national design competitions such as those for the Connective Corridor and From the Ground Up demonstrated models for such work.

The initiatives of UPSTATE: work in parallel with the building and landscape projects of the Near Westside Initiative (NWSI). Founded as a nonprofit development corporation by Syracuse University, it works intensively in one of the city's oldest neighborhoods under the aegis of the university's vice president for community engagement and economic development. The university was instrumental in providing $13.8 million through a state allocation as a nucleus for building acquisition and construction, with funds divided between the Syracuse University School of Architecture, the NWSI, and the Syracuse Center of Excellence (CoE), a state-funded facility dedicated to emerging technology. The resulting building and landscape projects on the Near Westside demonstrate the effectiveness of innovative design and energy systems paired with intense community engagement.

This collaboration created the context for From the Ground Up, a competition for high-performance homes organized in 2008 by

the Syracuse University School of Architecture in partnership with
the NWSI, the CoE, and Home HeadQuarters, a private not-for-profit
housing agency. The competition was initiated to support research
and development for energy-efficient homes that could accommodate
a variety of family types. It was also meant to encourage a reconsid-
eration of planning practices that have resulted in demolitions and
larger suburban lot sizes, eroding the character of Syracuse's walkable neighborhoods. The scale and the siting of the completed homes
retain neighborhood density, and the quality of the architecture heralds
welcome attention to the community (fig. 6).

This project also provides a microcosm of the complexity and constraints
of funding public work. Each source of subsidy to the housing provider
has limits associated with its use, from the time frame for expending
the funds to the income level of buyers. There are mandates for bidding,
for hiring, and for using green building materials. The Environmental
Protection Agency requires lead and asbestos abatement, and because
the project receives federal funding, any construction with a budget over
$25,000 must have licensed abatement teams.

In this mix of local and federal mandates, there is no legislated voice for
design as an essential component of the process. The funds and professional expertise of the School of Architecture help provide the impetus
for design at a more considered level. Innovations in design and
delivery can, for many reasons, end up being time- and labor-intensive
and can be viewed as a diversion from the core mission of providing

Fig. 6. Two high-performance
houses under construction
from the From the Ground Up
competition: left, R-House,
Architecture Research Office
and Della Valle Bernheimer; right,
TED House, Onion Flats, 2010

Fig. 7. The Syracuse Center of
Excellence in Environmental and
Energy Systems, Syracuse, New York.
Toshiko Mori Architect with Ashley
McGraw Architects, 2010

home ownership and neighborhood stability. Just as governmental regulations determine performance standards in a variety of categories, funding or other incentives effectively determine design standards where the market or legislation generally would not.

Risk and Reward

A creative team of disciplinary professionals is needed to navigate the intersections between commerce and the public good. The approach is not always a direct one, and the best responses can seem counterintuitive. The acclaimed design solutions for the Guggenheim Museum Bilbao, New York City's High Line, or Syracuse's Center of Excellence did not offer expected solutions in terms of form, program, or structure (fig. 7). Radical departures from standard practice are often necessary as cities are defined by speculation and regulation, heterogeneity and order, the familiar and the unexpected. This is not an argument for novelty but for something akin to art—the same creative leap that allows the sciences to progress, to innovate, and to seemingly make something out of nothing.

This is where legislation and bureaucracies, even well-intended ones, get lost. It is often beyond the available expertise of administrative offices to evaluate and quantify the impact of design proposals, so repetitions of earlier models are selected by default. A curatorial approach is required to effectively select designers and teams, just as a need for creative support is necessary throughout the administrative life of a project. Rather than a typical client's representative, whose sole emphasis is cost containment, an informed and influential voice like those that governed the Olympic Sculpture Park or the docklands redevelopment of Borneo-Sporenburg in Amsterdam is essential. These examples support the value of the design process, which includes synthetic thinking and multifaceted problem solving. They benefit from expanding "the limits of traditional methods that segregate designers from decision makers."[6]

The intentions of federally funded programs often achieve limited translation at the local level due to the complexity of public work. Threading through the multiple forces in play on a given site requires agility, which we as design educators endeavor to teach. These settings provide a bracing exposure for students and faculty.

The academy at its best sponsors experimentation, intellectual and aesthetic rigor—and risk. It does not exist to reproduce or simulate the market but to analyze it and perhaps, with that understanding, torque it—to introduce the market as just one more of our tools to accomplish better work. We cannot predict with exactitude what the future will look like or what its needs will be, but we can train students to respond to existing conditions with a projective optimism and skill.

The variety of projects in Syracuse, both in the studio and in the city, has affected urban design with relative speed. They model the way in which scarce funds can be allocated to accomplish work on multiple fronts that are economic, environmental, and social. Much of what has been suggested and implemented in Syracuse has been successfully implemented in other cities over the past forty years. For example, infill strategies that create mixed residential and commercial centers with universities as anchors in public/private partnerships have been developed at the campus perimeters of institutions such as Ohio State University and the University of Pennsylvania. Syracuse University and the city of Syracuse have the ability to test and implement innovative strategies in mix and type that are integrated with connective infrastructure.

The catalog of public work in other cities here and abroad offers an array of approaches that can be instructive to business and political leaders. This is not to suggest that precedents can be adopted in full by another city any more than a single-bullet solution—like an entertainment zone, festival market, stadium, or mall—can provide an economic and civic panacea. Specific work grows from the context. In order for leadership to be effective it needs to be informed and able to better make the case for investment. The knowledge rests in many areas, and in order to accomplish this, coalitions are necessary. Alliances demand often-unexpected affiliations across academic and civic groups and draw on a wide array of advocates. Trust and social capital as well as funding and expertise permit the realization of future work that is often unfamiliar and difficult.

As we have seen with past economic crashes and oil shortages, crises get our attention, and we mobilize in response to cataclysmic rather than chronic circumstances. Radical shifts justify equally radical responses and can help garner support for change and adjustments in behavior at the local and state levels. Our choices of goals and the way in which these are translated from the highest levels are significant. In the end, if economic stimulus only provides temporary jobs and is not part of a larger set of intentions, the benefits end with the specific funding. The disruption of a crisis can be managed; what follows is an opportunity for new thinking and new proposals. A critical response in crisis can have lasting impact.

The development of cities takes many hands. The projects in Syracuse are evidence of the creative drive and commitment of many individuals. Valued partners and colleagues include Marilyn Higgins, vice president for community engagement and economic development; Kerry Quaglia, executive director of Home HeadQuarters; Ed Bogusz, executive director of the Center of Excellence; Eric Beattie, director of campus planning, design, and construction; Julia Czerniak, director of UPSTATE:; Mayor Stephanie Miner; and Paul Driscoll, commissioner, Department of Neighborhood and Business Development. This work has been made possible only within the supportive framework at the university created by the dynamic vision of Chancellor Nancy Cantor.

1   Roger Runningen, "Obama's $50 Billion Spending Plan to Boost Economy, Report Says," *Bloomberg*, October 11, 2010, http://www.bloomberg.com/news/2010-10-11/obama-s-50-billion-transportation-plan-would-boost-economy-report-says.html.

2   Mark Wiener, "Former Rep. James Walsh, Once a King of Pork, Now Backs Reform of Earmarks," *Post-Standard*, September 29, 2010.

3   Paul Driscoll, commissioner of neighborhood and business development, Syracuse, New York.

4   The city's Community Development Block Grant funding is now at the lowest point in its thirty-eight-year history, at roughly a third of its height of $18 million in the 1980s, according to Driscoll.

5   The university has, at various points in its history, held properties in downtown Syracuse and on the apron of campus.

6   Design-Related Research Analysis and Planning Study, ARO, HR&A, and Mark Robbins, 2011. Unpublished draft of a design study on federal design excellence commissioned by the General Service Administration and the National Endowment for the Arts.

Cleveland:
Medi-Plex City
McLain
Clutter

Fig. 1. The Cleveland Clinic's new
Sydell and Arnold Miller Family
Pavilion, July 23, 2010

Prologue

It is 8 a.m. on July 23, 2010. We are in the front lobby of the Cleveland
Clinic's new $634 million Sydell and Arnold Miller Family Pavilion.
The building is immense—1.3 million square feet—and starkly
neomodern. Its first floor is composed of a series of linked and spatially
dynamic lobbies, three and four stories in height, all finished in sleek
white terrazzo floors and flawless plaster walls with stainless steel,
walnut, and frosted glass accents. The lobbies compose a city within
the city, with coffee shops, restaurants, newsstands, clothing stores,
places of worship, and offices lining their length. The walls are adorned
with a modern-art collection that would be the envy of many American
museums, and on Saturdays a harpist takes her seat near the front entry,
gently plucking elegantly distributed notes for passersby. On other
days, carefully engineered New Age tones are pumped throughout
the facility through cunningly hidden speakers. The music is funda-
mentally sympathetic. Had your loved one died today, you would feel
soothed. Had he or she survived a complicated procedure, you would
feel appropriately encouraged. Stewards in sporting red jackets litter
the lobbies waiting to direct you, and genius doctors whiz to and fro
in pairs wearing crisp white coats. Gone since July 21 is the motorcade
of black Hummers with New York plates that had circled the facility's
valet drop-off for the past several weeks. The Saudi princess whom they
accompanied has returned home following her successful heart trans-
plant. Present, still, are a few African and European continentals, mixed
with the occasional Amish in beard and overalls. Upstairs, professionals
are pushing the limits of medical science—inventing new and extended

states of human life. Somewhere within the hospital is one of many ICUs, linked to this lobby via a labyrinthine series of corridors, elevators, tunnels, and bridges.[1] Within the unit is a Connecticut woman whose face was famously consumed by a 200-pound chimpanzee. Her face will be restored; the chimp was destroyed. In November, she will be visited by Oprah. The building is an antiseptic volume of abstract space, housing surreal and unlikely contrasts assembled from an international palette. Despite the best efforts of its designers to soothe the occupants through every possible aesthetic and sensory accompaniment, an underlying and barely palpable tension is ever present to the astute. On this day, the tension is amplified. The lobby seems starved of oxygen, balanced on a needle. In a few hours, President Obama will visit. He will not touch Cleveland's ground. He will arrive via air, landing on one of the Clinic's helipads. He will then be ushered through the hospital's interior. Stumping for American health-care reform, he is visiting the Cleveland Clinic to affirm the suspicion of almost everyone who visits the Sydell and Arnold Miller Family Pavilion: this is the hospital of the future (fig. 1).

Outside, the hum of an electric bus is barely audible on the newly constructed HealthLine along Euclid Avenue. The bus connects the Clinic's main campus to downtown and a series of hotels built to house the hospital's visitors. Along its route, the bus traverses block upon block of vacant and decaying urban land (fig. 2). On any given day, a passenger on the HealthLine might observe the Clinic's sprawl amidst the surrounding urban decay and provide a diagnosis. It might seem

Fig. 2. Sequence along the Euclid Avenue HealthLine from downtown to the Cleveland Clinic

clear enough that the city is dying. The Clinic is spreading like a cancer, seizing the opportunity to expand in the city's wake. The hospital is growing in patterns of development more similar to an exurban office park than recognizable urbanism. In this sense, the acres of territory occupied by the Clinic might appropriately be labeled "formerly urban."

But such a diagnosis would misrecognize a latent opportunity. Within the Clinic's lobbies is a glimmer of a kind of urbanism. The unlikely diversity of constituency indexes the semblance of the international metropolis; the Clinic's restaurants, clothing stores, and entertainment venues are characteristic of the contemporary neoliberal city; the sheer density of circulation in the Clinic's lobbies recalls the early twentieth-century street. To be sure, these are not models to be accepted without criticism—but they are urban nonetheless.

A more careful diagnosis of the relationship between Cleveland and the Clinic is needed. Such an analysis would prove useful throughout the Rust Belt, for cities such as Pittsburgh, Toledo, and Buffalo, to name just a few. These cities share with Cleveland a faltering industrial past and a booming medical industry that now ranks among their top employers. By parsing the relationship between Cleveland and its clinic—by examining the causes of this contrast between surreal activity within the Clinic's lobbies and its blighted surroundings—this analysis may serve as a case study for investigation of other postindustrial cities, reframing their relationship with the medical industry in order to project a new urban future.

Cleveland's Rise and Fall
Cleveland was once the fourth-largest city in the United States. The city first rose to prominence in the late nineteenth century as a major port for goods flowing into the Great Lakes through the Ohio and Erie Canal, and in the early twentieth century its status as a major American city solidified as it developed into a critical manufacturing center along railway networks linking the Rust Belt to the East Coast (fig. 3). But as the industrial sector—the historic economic foundation of Cleveland— became increasingly tenuous, the city lapsed into decades of sustained decline. Complicating the loss of the city's economic base, the mid-century exodus of the middle class that afflicted most American cities had an immense impact on Cleveland. While many cities have recovered from this demographic shift, Cleveland's population has continued to decrease for six decades. This loss of industry and population has left a gap in Cleveland's tax base that has yet to be filled.

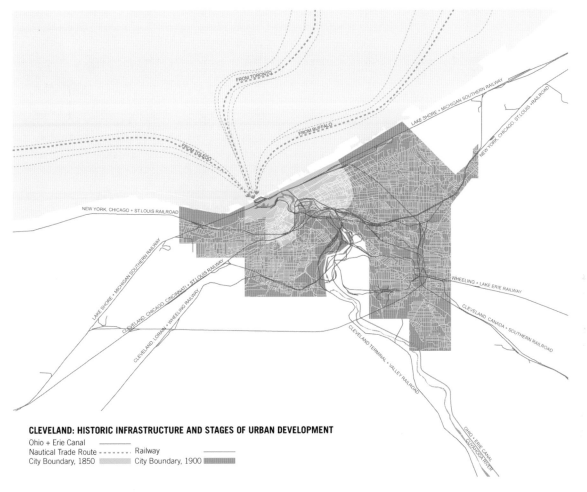

CLEVELAND: HISTORIC INFRASTRUCTURE AND STAGES OF URBAN DEVELOPMENT
Ohio + Erie Canal
Nautical Trade Route -------- Railway
City Boundary, 1850   City Boundary, 1900

Attendant to Cleveland's demographic and economic decline has been the increasingly dire state of its built environment. Despite a much-touted attempt to revitalize downtown in the 1990s and early adoption of creative planning strategies like land banking, Cleveland is increasingly scarred with vast swaths of urban blight and acres of vacant property (fig. 4).[2] Much of this land requires remediation due to the city's industrial past. In recent years the nation's housing crisis has amplified Cleveland's vacancy problems, as the kind of high-risk mortgages that largely account for defaults unevenly targeted the low-income demographic composing the city's population. In many ways, Cleveland seems poised to fade from existence. Following the lead of its regional neighbors like Detroit and Flint, one strategy for Cleveland's future might be strategic erasure, allowing the city to gracefully and slowly excise itself from existence.

Fig. 3. Cleveland's historic development and infrastructure

VACANT LAND
Downtown   ✕
Cleveland Clinic   ✕

Fig. 4. Vacant land
in Cleveland

Amidst this perfect storm of bad news, one sector of the city's economy
has been growing prodigiously: health care.[3] As factories and warehouses have fallen, hospitals and health-care facilities have sprung
up en masse. And in Cleveland, health care is synonymous with the
Cleveland Clinic, the city's world-class namesake. The Clinic was
founded in 1921 during Cleveland's industrial ascent; its first building
was erected within the boundary of its current campus on the city's
East Side. At its inception, the privately held nonprofit had a dual
purpose: to serve the population of its quickly growing city and to
operate as a research facility that would broaden medical knowledge
at large. These motives were memorialized in the Clinic's often quoted
founding mission statement, committing the hospital to "better care
of the sick, investigation into their problems, and further education
of those who serve."

It was the Clinic's latter commitment, to research, that sparked rapid growth in the hospital. The Clinic became a national leader in several branches of specialized medicine by mid-century, and its research agenda continued to fuel its growth even in the last several decades, despite the woes of its host city. This fortitude has guided the hospital to develop a much more complex relationship with Cleveland than that expressed in its founding mission statement—one that is rife with interrelated economic, aesthetic, and ideological issues, and one that might reestablish Cleveland's prominence as a critical node in larger economic networks.

Cleveland and the Clinic

Today, the Clinic is easily Cleveland's most robust economic juggernaut. Topping industrial stalwarts like Ford Motor Company and LTV Steel, the hospital is now the metropolitan area's largest employer.[4] A 2010 economic impact report found that the Clinic was responsible for nearly 8 percent of the Cleveland metropolitan area's regional economy, contributing $10.5 billion.[5] The hospital was responsible for 81,000 jobs, amounting to $3.9 billion in wages and $648 million in local and state income taxes. Recalling twentieth-century company towns built around factories, 56,000 households in the Cleveland metropolitan area are supported by the Clinic, adding $2.2 billion of household spending to the local economy.[6] In a city with a population that now barely tops 400,000 residents, the hospital's contribution is significant. The Clinic has become a cornerstone of the regional economy.

For decades, a significant portion of the Clinic's revenue has come from a boutique sector of the medical industry now known as "medical tourism." Most commonly characterized by Western patients flying overseas to locations in India or Thailand for cheap surgeries, the Clinic is one of a few Western hospitals that capitalize on the reversal of this phenomenon. Regional and national patients visit the Cleveland Clinic by the thousands for care. Even international patients, drawn from other wealthy nations like Saudi Arabia, travel to the hospital for cutting-edge treatment. Since 1975 medical tourists have been guided through the process of visiting Cleveland for complex medical procedures by the Clinic's Global Patient Services department, where employees speak thirteen different languages.[7] In 2009, 25 percent of the Clinic's patients came from outside Cleveland's seven-county region, including nearly 10 percent from sixty-two different countries.[8]

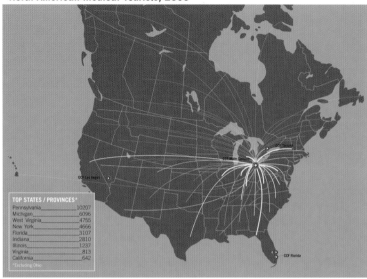

North American Medical Tourists, 2009

TOP STATES / PROVINCES*	
Pennsylvania	10207
Michigan	6096
West Virginia	4755
New York	4666
Florida	3107
Indiana	2810
Illinois	1237
Virginia	813
California	642
*Excluding Ohio	

Fig. 5. Domestic medical tourism at the Cleveland Clinic

Fig. 6. International medical tourism at the Cleveland Clinic

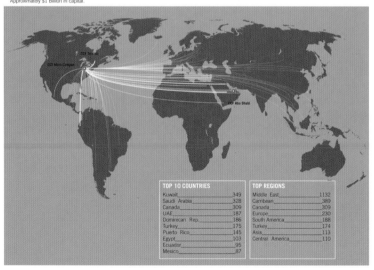

International Medical Tourists, 2009

2761 International Patients from 102 Different Countries.
Approximately $1 Billion in capital.

TOP 10 COUNTRIES		TOP REGIONS	
Kuwait	349	Middle East	1132
Saudi Arabia	328	Caribbean	389
Canada	309	Canada	309
UAE	187	Europe	230
Dominican Rep.	186	South America	188
Turkey	175	Turkey	174
Puerto Rico	145	Asia	113
Egypt	103	Central America	110
Ecuador	95		
Mexico	87		

The Clinic does not publicize its revenues from medical tourism, but a conservative estimate would place their annual income near $1.5 billion.[9] When one considers that international patients pay out of pocket, without the benefit of the negotiated rates offered by insurance companies, total revenues could be much higher. The Cleveland Clinic has become a formidable condenser of regional, national, and global flows of capital in the medical industry. Echoing the city's history as an important point of trade for goods traveling from the Atlantic Ocean into the Great Lakes, the Clinic's medical tourism activity links Cleveland to a global network of capital and commerce (figs. 5, 6).

The Clinic's economic success is most clearly legible in its aggressive building campaign on the city's East Side. Occupying an expanding region between downtown and Cleveland's University Circle neighborhood, along a stretch of Euclid Avenue once home to wealthy industrialists, the Clinic's compound now covers more than 500 acres of urban land—this, despite the epic decline of the surrounding neighborhood, where an increasing amount of property is falling vacant and dormant. The dormant land surrounding the Clinic provides an ideal fit for the spatial needs of a contemporary medical institution. Commonly relegated to suburban office parks or edge-city campuses, the contemporary hospital is most suited for sites evacuated of locational specificity. Like a shopping mall, cutting-edge medical facilities draw little from their contexts, resting on the land like massive spacecrafts visiting earth only long enough to board passengers. Their interiors evince an aura of international spatial neutrality—placeless and self-similar regardless of their environs.[10]

Fig. 7. Spatial neutrality and placelessness

The property surrounding the Clinic complements the hospital's placelessness. The land was deforested and stripped of natural attributes by years of industrial and residential land uses, and then stripped of evidence of those uses by years of decay and disinvestment. The property is flat, beige, and nearly featureless (fig. 7). The abundance of this property has made it possible for the Clinic to choose to expand within the city limits. Indeed, the Clinic's development seems to have achieved a kind of inverse ratio to the surrounding blight, at times apparently catalyzed by the city's decline. As the neighborhood's historic fabric and economic foundation fail, and the local government is unable to stem the blight, the Clinic's vitality places the hospital in a unique position to occupy and remediate vast swaths of dormant property. In 2010, in the face of continuing economic downturn in the United States, the Clinic has committed to spending an additional $840 million in capital development in the region.[11] As a point of comparison, Cleveland's 2010 general fund budget, which supports all basic civic services and offices, was only $501 million.[12]

Despite its massive economic contribution, the Clinic's relationship with Cleveland and its reflection on the built environment should not go unexamined. As a legally classified charitable organization, the

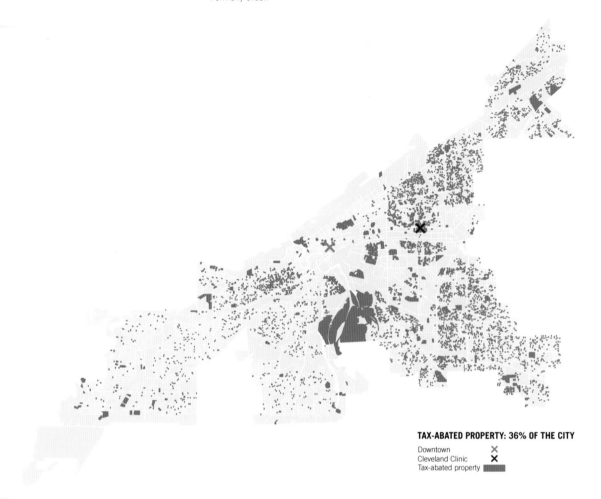

TAX-ABATED PROPERTY: 36% OF THE CITY

Downtown ⨯
Cleveland Clinic ✕
Tax-abated property ▮▮▮▮▮▮

Fig. 8. Tax-abated property in Cleveland

hospital holds itself in a curious state of exception from the surrounding city.[13] It may capitalize on the ready availability and affordability of property to expand its complex, but once it has occupied this property it is exempt from paying property tax. City programs such as the Vacant Property Initiative (VPI), which grants loans to corporations for developing vacant urban land, have aided in the Clinic's sprawl.[14] But once the Clinic has occupied VPI property, it holds these lands economically off the grid in terms of taxation.[15] In 2009, tax-abated property accounted for a stunning 36 percent of the real estate in the city of Cleveland (fig. 8). Two nonprofit institutions, the Cleveland Clinic and University Hospitals, account for the majority of this property. In 2009 alone, nonprofits occupied land that would have netted local governments and school districts an additional $34 million in taxes had they been held by a for-profit organization.[16]

Advocates of the Clinic note that the hospital's waived property taxes are more than accounted for through donations granted to urban organizations and sectors of the local government. As is required of a tax-exempt nonprofit institution, the Clinic must demonstrate its contribution to society. The hospital does this, in part, through charitable donations; in 2008, the Clinic donated more than $86 million.[17] The Clinic also reported that it administered over $200 million worth of charitable care to the poor and uninsured.[18] Indeed, these contributions well exceed the lost revenues from property tax, and secure the Clinic as one of the most generous philanthropic entities in the Cleveland metropolitan area. Many of these donations went to cultural institutions like the Cleveland Museum of Art, but other benefactors included programs typically supported through tax revenues like the Greater Cleveland Rapid Transit Authority and the city school district, which the hospital granted over $1 million.[19]

But the Clinic's philanthropy cannot be fully characterized by generosity. The institution's tax-exempt status places the hospital in a position to choose what urban programs or branches of government to support—certainly a privilege that tax-paying institutions never directly experience. Beyond benign contributions to basic city services and cultural institutions, the Clinic granted funds to organizations with overt political agendas, such as the conservative Brookings Institution. And the hospital's single largest benefactor, receiving over $16 million, was its own subsidiary—the Cleveland Clinic Educational Foundation.[20] The Clinic is in an economic position to grant funds to urban programs and public offices in amounts that rival, or even surpass, those granted by the local government. In doing so, it challenges the agency of the city's elected government to determine Cleveland's future, and builds political alliances that further aid its expanding power in the region.

One might wonder why Cleveland would not attempt to curb the growth of an entity that removes so much property from its tax base. The answer may lie in Cleveland's tax structure. Significantly, Cleveland property tax accounted for only 8 percent of the city's revenues in 2010, while income tax accounted for 51 percent.[21] This is an unusually high percentage of a city's budget to be contributed by income tax, and the Cleveland Clinic's immense work force is certainly a large contributor to this figure.[22] The Clinic's relationship to this tax structure further clarifies its symbiosis with Cleveland's expanding blight. The Clinic may expand freely due to urban decay, low property values, and its tax-abated status, and the city encourages this expansion

Opposite: Fig. 9. A sequence
of interior conditioned spaces

through zoning concessions because its operating budget is primarily based on income tax. Were the city to resist the Clinic's expansion, it would curtail the growth of a significant contributor to the single largest line item in Cleveland's revenue stream. In light of this, far from resisting the Clinic's expansion, Cleveland is actively promoting the facility's growth. Working with Cuyahoga County, the Clinic, and a handful of related medical and research enterprises, the Cleveland City Planning Commission has recently created three special development regions that comprise the Cleveland Health-Tech Corridor.[23] These zoning districts encompass approximately 4.5 miles of Euclid Avenue between downtown Cleveland and University Circle and reportedly will give carte blanche to the Clinic and its associated medical institutions to grow at will. These special zoning districts reflect the fact that, in effect, the city's revenue structure is *contingent* on urban blight, which allows institutions like the Clinic to grow liberally. Under its current tax structure, blight is one of Cleveland's most valuable assets.

Granted an environment conducive to liberal growth, the manner in which the Clinic develops the city is laden with ideological content. By their nature, urban hospitals have a complex relationship with the cities in which they are sited. Resistant to complete assimilation into an urban organization, hospitals come attendant with their own disciplinary protocols of classification and exclusion.[24] They form heterotopic urban enclaves: prohibitive megablocks with complex internal quasi-urbanisms, or dendritic tangles of buildings strung block to block by pedestrian bridges and subterranean passages. These complexes engage their host cities strategically and minimally by channeling traffic flows into parking structures and admitting patients and goods through restricted access corridors. Critical patients and time-sensitive biological tissues avoid ground-level engagement entirely, arriving via Life Flight through invisible corridors of regional and urban airspace. By necessity, urban hospitals filter and edit their surrounding cities as they do disease and pathogens floating through the air.[25]

The Clinic could serve as an object lesson of these phenomena. It is nominally sited in Cleveland, as might be an airport or an international bank whose conceptual locality is as much in global infrastructural routes or ephemeral flows of capital as in its physical city. Certainly, the Clinic engages Cleveland in a selective fashion. Its campus spans over what was once sixty city blocks, often depositing megabuildings that straddle several historic streets. Medical buildings, research facilities, parking structures, and hotels wind and contort their way between

existing structures, shaping themselves in a negotiation between maximum site coverage and interior functional protocols. They create a shotgun spray of facilities across a large swath of the city, and are connected via tunnels and overhead bridges. City streets are sometimes removed, segmented, or privatized as service drives. Read together with the bridges and tunnels, they create a discontinuous tartan that reads like an aberration of the surrounding urban grid. Recent master planning on the campus has integrated a series of quadrangles and courtyards—a strategy borrowed, of course, from collegiate campus design. But at the Clinic, the latent history of this landscape typology becomes blatantly evident. The quads are exclusionary anesthetized exteriors, excised from the surrounding urban space and made to answer exclusively to the protocols of the buildings that define them. Some are overmanicured and prohibit easy use, existing only to give lobby occupants something to look out at—*anything* other than the surrounding city. Walk along a city street inside the campus, and you will find yourself a minority. Walk along a street outside the campus, and you will find yourself absolutely alone. Every aspect of the Clinic's designed relationship to the surrounding city announces the campus's exclusivity and excision.

This uneasy relationship between the Clinic and its host city accounts for what could be an otherworldly visit for the medical tourist. A patient might fly out of Dubai, arrive at Cleveland Hopkins Airport, enter a limo, and be driven to a Clinic building for admission—thus beginning a several-month hospital stay that could include medical services in facilities across a large portion of the city, without ever stepping foot outside a building. One might be admitted through the emergency building, be moved two elevators, several corridors, and two bridges away to the G Building for surgery, then venture a similar journey to an ICU in the J Building for post-op, and so on. The hospital complex is packed with similar routes, continuities of interior conditioned space layered blindly over the dying city below (fig. 9). Family members of a patient might take up long-term residence in a Clinic-affiliated hotel and commute back and forth daily on the HealthLine, whose buses occupy a designated lane of Euclid Avenue—again, remaining strangely isolated from the surrounding city.

Hence, the Clinic has developed a complex coexistence with its city. It collects capital from global, national, and regional sources, making itself uniquely vital and essential in the contexts of Cleveland's faltering economy. Because it is such an essential economic benefactor to the city, it is afforded an environment that is extremely conducive to liberal and unchecked growth. As it grows, it removes urban property from the tax base, making the Clinic's substantial economic impact an even more essential part of the region's future, while forging a unique symbiosis with the city's urban blight.[26] Meanwhile, the character of the Clinic's development reiterates an aura of passivity upon Cleveland's urban environment. Excised from the surrounding city while expanding in bulk, the Clinic's complex amounts to an incredibly present absence in urban development—a massive index of Cleveland's urban past.

Toward the Medi-Plex City

One response to the issues raised by the Clinic's unchecked growth in Cleveland might be to resist the hospital's continued expansion. Given the Clinic's tremendous economic contribution to the Cleveland metropolitan area, however, this response seems extremely unwise. The medical industry and its attendant flow of international, national, and regional capital is one of the few points of hope for Cleveland. Instead, a more pragmatic response might call for a critically rene- gotiated relationship between the Clinic and the city. For guidance, we might look to one of our best historians on the emergence of the hospital as an urban type, Michel Foucault.

The hospital, for Foucault, was an important model in his study of the disciplinary society, a social structure in which power and knowledge are embodied in designed relationships between individuals in space or in the spatialization of surveillance and observation. The disciplinary society is characterized by the productive organization in space of previously unvariegated masses of humanity. Prior to the emergence of this social organization, the concept of the hospital as an institution for rehabilitation did not exist. In its place were asylums in which the ill, as a mass, were quarantined and prevented from infecting the populace. Accordingly, these asylums were made exclusive and sealed off from their surrounding cities.

Foucault theorized that the disciplinary society brought to these prede- cessors of the early modern hospital the spatial culture to individuate, organize, and survey patients and their various illnesses. Early hospitals emerged as a product of the spatial logic of the disciplinary society, as they discursively engaged their contemporary developments in medical science. Hence, critically, the hospital was both *symptomatic* and *consti- tutive* of the disciplinary society and its attendant production of power and knowledge.[27] The hospital was both a product and a producer of

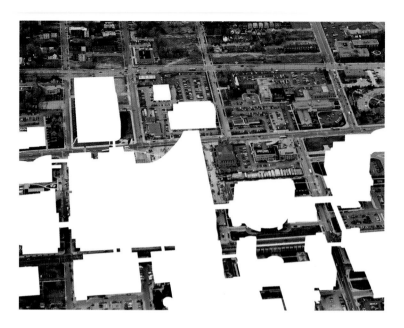

Fig. 10. The Cleveland Clinic

society. With the rise of the early modern hospital came a new relationship between the institution and the city. The disciplinary society
positioned the hospital, no longer an exception to the surrounding
urbanism, to be an urban actor. Foucault wrote, "The location of the
hospital had to be determined within the overall medicine of urban
space."[28] Thus, the spatial protocols of the hospital were engaged
with those of the city at large, and participated within the disciplinary
regime of the city and its attendant production of social structures.[29]

As it stands today, the Clinic exists as a kind of a heterotopic city resting
atop a dying city—interiorized and resistant to assimilation into a larger
urban culture (fig. 10). At least at first glance, the Clinic seems to have
reverted to the exclusivity characteristic of the hospital's predecessor,
the asylum. No doubt, this is largely because hospitals need to be exclusionary in order to satisfy their hygienic and clinical functions. But,
paradoxically, Foucault's analysis argues that hospitals, despite their
necessary exclusivity, are productive of urban society and subjectivities.
In Foucault's account, the functional protocols of the hospital and the
way these protocols shaped the institution's organization were coexis-
tent and complementary to the disciplining of space within the city at
large. Viewed through this lens, the Clinic—an institution governed by
abundant spatial protocols—seems poised to be a more active partici-
pant in its surrounding urbanism.

In the Cleveland Clinic, we find facilities that are extremely specific in their instrumentalization of the technological and spatial protocols of the contemporary hospital, and an institution whose interface with the space of the city is equally mediated through a series of economic factors. Recalling the July 2010 day described at the beginning of this text, we also find the influx of a kind of surreal diversity that is often attendant to a vital contemporary metropolis. What Foucault's insight might lead a designer to consider is how these two qualities of the Clinic—its abundance of spatial logics and the broad cross section of public constituencies and events it houses—might be put in chorus. In other words, how might the spatial protocols of the Clinic be brought to bear on the way the hospital organizes, combines, and recombines the constituencies it gathers and the public events it sponsors? How, too, might this diagram become more broadly solicitous of interaction with Cleveland's public at large? It might mean, for example, designing courtyards that serve as space for the Clinic's staff and visitors as well as public space for the surrounding urban population. Or it might mean networking the commerce in the interior urbanism of the Clinic's lobbies with systems of shopping across the city at large. Or it might mean atomizing hospital departments and developing strategies to interface and graft them into urban programs. These examples are perhaps reductive, and to be sure, any design intervention would need to be accompanied by policy and incentives that would allow the Clinic to rethink its development methods. Nevertheless, the effects of this kind of design thinking could be profound.

Through such a design methodology, the Clinic's current symbiosis with Cleveland's urban blight might be refigured to yield other productive, symbiotic relationships—spatial, economic, and social. This would be a tactical urbanism, a careful negotiation between city and hospital. And, critically, Foucault's analysis reveals the broad intellectual territory that these kinds of design tactics would engage. Recasting the theorists' analysis of the discourse between the spatialities of the early modern hospital and its surrounding urbanism as a projective ambition for the relationship between the contemporary medical complex and its host city, this kind of design method could lead to new kinds of urban social structures, civic life, and even medical knowledge.

Such a strategy for urban development would certainly prove beneficial for Cleveland. It would also be a useful case study for Cleveland's regional neighbors throughout the Rust Belt. Like Cleveland, these cities are striving to rebuild their urban and economic fabric in the wake of their industrial pasts.

1   Such continuities of interior conditioned space are reminiscent of what Rem Koolhaas has
     called "junkspace." See Rem Koolhaas, "Junkspace," *October* 100 (Spring 2002): 175–90.

2   "Cleveland Revives Blighted Neighborhoods by Easing Bureaucracy on Vacant Land,"
     Philadelphia Inquirer, November 30, 2001.

3   For example, see Steven Prokesch, "Cleveland Counts on a Clinic," *New York Times*,
     December 29, 1986.

4   The Clinic was the largest employer in Cleveland as early as 1986. See Prokesch,
     "Cleveland Counts on a Clinic." For more recent accounts, see also America's Career
     InfoNet, "State Profile: Largest Employers, Ohio," 2007.

5   Cleveland Clinic, "Cleveland Clinic: A Vital Force in Ohio's Economy," May 4, 2011,
     http://my.clevelandclinic.org/media_relations/library/2011/2011_05_04_cleveland_clinic_vital_
     force_in_ohios_economy.aspx.

6   Cleveland Clinic, "A Vital Force in Ohio's Economy (Economic Impact Report)," 2010.

7   Cayla Lambier, "American Hospitality—Inbound Medical Tourism at International Standards,"
     Medical Tourism Magazine, August 4, 2009, http://www.medicaltourismmag.com/article/
     American-Hospitality.html.

8   Sarah Jane Tribble, "Cleveland Clinic Continues Expansion Despite Recession," *Plain Dealer*,
     February 25, 2010.

9   Author's estimate, based on published numbers of international patients and reported
     revenue of $5.57 billion in 2009. See Tribble, "Cleveland Clinic Continues Expansion
     Despite Recession."

10   Like a commercial franchise, the contemporary hospital often neutralizes geographic
     difference through the recitation of vaguely familiar architectural styles. Similarly,
     it neutralizes differences between the various subjectivities in its halls by evenly labeling
     them either "patient" or "visitor." In these ways, the contemporary hospital resembles what
     Marc Augé has labeled the "non-place." See Marc Augé, *Non-places: Introduction to an
     Anthropology of Supermodernity*, trans. John Howe (New York and London: Verso, 1995).

11   Tribble, "Cleveland Clinic Continues Expansion Despite Recession."

12   The general fund supports police and fire protection, emergency medical services, waste
     collection, recreation, health centers, park maintenance, building and housing regulation,
     and municipal courts. The city's capital budget is not reported or tabulated, as it often
     draws from complex credit lines from the state and public–private partnerships.
     See Frank G. Jackson and the Committee on Finance, *City of Cleveland 2010 Budget Book*,
     March, 29, 2010.

13   In many ways, the Clinic's campus can be productively compared with what Giorgio
     Agamben has called a camp, a territory of juridical and spatial exception. See Giorgio
     Agamben, *Homo Sacer: Sovereign Power and Bare Life*, trans. Daniel Heller-Roazen
     (Stanford, Calif.: Stanford University Press, 1998), 166–88.

14   City of Cleveland Department of Economic Development, "Report to Council, 2010."

15   In Cleveland, property taxes are paid to Cuyahoga County, which then distributes funds
     to municipal governments and offices. The largest benefactor is the Cleveland Municipal
     School District, followed by the city of Cleveland, and then the county.

16   Zach Schiller to Jim Rokakis, memorandum, 17 December 2009, in *Policy Matters Ohio*
     (Cleveland, Ohio: Policy Matters, 2009).

17   Cleveland Clinic, IRS Form 990, 2008.

18   Of course, this number should be weighed against the inevitable overall inflation of
      health-care costs to balance expenses resulting from treatment to those who cannot pay.
      See Cleveland Clinic, IRS Form 990.

19   Cleveland Clinic, IRS Form 990.

20   Ibid.

21   It must be noted that in 2010, property tax accounted for only 8 percent of Cleveland's
      $507.4 million in revenues. Income tax, of which the Clinic is a major contributor,
      accounted for 51 percent. However, this distribution of revenue is not necessarily typical,
      and certainly not reflective of a vital city. In Chicago, income tax accounts for only 7.5
      percent of tax revenues. See Jackson, *City of Cleveland 2010 Budget Book*; and City of
      Chicago, *Corporate Fund Summary, 2009 Year-End Estimate*.

22   In more vital cities, like New York, property tax accounts for more than three times the
      amount of revenue accrued through income tax. Even in more comparable cities, like
      Pittsburgh, property tax is commonly double the income tax revenues. See City of
      New York, *Adopted Budget Fiscal Year 2011*; and City of Pittsburgh, *2010 Budget*.

23   Cleveland Health-Tech Corridor, http://www.healthtechcorridor.com/.

24   Michel Foucault, "The Incorporation of the Hospital into Modern Technology," in *Space,
      Knowledge and Power: Foucault and Geography*, ed. Jeremy W. Crampton and Stuart Elden
      (Aldershot, U.K.: Ashgate, 2007), 143.

25   Hilary Sample has recently made a similar argument. See Hilary Sample, "Biomed City,"
      in *Verb Crisis* (Barcelona and New York: Actar, 2008), 72.

26   It should be noted that the kind of vacant land the Clinic appropriates is of low value,
      thus netting little or no taxable income. Similar property is often land-banked by the
      county, also netting no property tax revenues. However, the city's relationship with the
      Clinic invests in a future where the property will never be taxable.

27   Foucault, "The Incorporation of the Hospital into Modern Technology," 143–48.

28   Ibid., 149.

29   Foucault's thoughts have since been revised, noting that in late capitalism, social relations
      are enforced equally through ephemeral systems, like credit, as through urban spatiality.
      For example, see Gilles Deleuze, "Postscript on the Societies of Control," *October* 59
      (Winter 1992): 3–7. Indeed, even a quick assessment of the contemporary condition would
      reveal social regimes that are far too placeless, overlapping, and nimble to abide by
      Foucault's analysis.

Lessons Learned from a Shrinking City: Youngstown 2010 and Beyond

Hunter Morrison

Introduction

Across America's Great Lakes region, once proud and prosperous industrial cities have seen their economic base erode or disappear entirely, their working-class neighborhoods decay, their compact downtowns die, and their civic institutions struggle to stay solvent. Cities from Youngstown and Flint to St. Louis and Detroit have seen their peak population drop by over 50 percent, while other cities throughout the region have experienced smaller, though no less destructive, losses. Reinventing these cities as smaller, greener, more equitable places that can prosper once again presents a challenge not only for the Great Lakes region but also for the United States as a whole.

This binational region surrounds the Great Lakes and spans from the western slopes of the Appalachian Mountains to the Upper Mississippi. For over a hundred years—from the beginning of the Civil War to the end of the Vietnam War—this region led the nation in industrial production. The region attracted people from all over the world to work in the mills and factories that drove the growth of its great industrial cities. During World War II, these cities—led by Detroit—became known as "the Arsenal of Democracy," as they converted production from consumer goods to the planes, ships, tanks, and other armaments that eventually overwhelmed the Axis forces. After the war, as its factories pivoted back to consumer markets, these cities fed the nation's insatiable thirst for the sleek cars and modern appliances that came to define the good life in America's ever-expanding suburbs.

The end of the region's industrial hegemony began quietly in the 1960s and 1970s and accelerated in the early 1980s. As employment declined, so did the immigration of large numbers of low-skilled people to work in its factories and live in its city neighborhoods, while the exodus of city residents who could leave for the suburbs increased.

As a consequence of these trends, Great Lakes cities experienced unprecedented levels of population decline. Of the nation's twenty-three larger cities (with populations over 60,000) that have lost one-third or more of their peak-level population, 70 percent are in the Great Lakes region. Of the twelve American cities that have lost over 40 percent of their peak-level population, all but New Orleans are in the Great Lakes region. Six cities—all in the Great Lakes—have lost over 50 percent of their peak population: St. Louis (62.7 percent), Youngstown (60.6 percent), Pittsburgh (54.8 percent), Buffalo (55 percent), Cleveland (56.6 percent), and Detroit (61.4 percent).

Loss of this magnitude has challenged planners and politicians as well as the public to confront the harsh realities both that their industrial past is gone and that the way ahead is difficult and uncertain. In the future, the region's ability to compete globally and, in the face of the projected increase in the nation's population, to urbanize sustainably will depend, in large part, on how its historically industrial communities address their legacy liabilities—such as brownfields, widespread abandonment and disinvestment, and low educational attainment and economic exclusion based on race and class. The long-term health of the Great Lakes region will depend as well on how its communities take advantage of their legacy assets—such as universities, hospitals, parks, fine-arts institutions, historic neighborhoods, industrial-strength infrastructure, and the entrepreneurial spirit of a practical people—to shape a new, more promising future.

Americans have long associated the size of a city's population with its vitality and importance as a place. As a nation we conflate growth with prosperity and shrinkage with decline, and are too often willing to write off whole cities as dying and disposable because they are no longer growing. As a consequence, public officials have found it difficult to discuss with their constituents the profound impacts of persistent population loss and economic disinvestment; to do so risks admitting failure. At the same time, planners and allied design professionals have struggled to address decline of scale. Sadly, they have received little support from their national professional associations. Professional interest and energies flow in the opposite direction, under the banners of "new urbanism," "smart growth," and "sustainable development." As Philipp Oswalt, director of the "Shrinking Cities" project of the Kulturstiftung des Bundes in Germany, has observed, "faced with the phenomenon of shrinkage, urban planning is merely reactive because… it has little influence on…deindustrialization, demographic change, or even suburbanization."[1] Simply put, the challenge facing these depopulating communities and the professionals working in them is one of managing change rather than of managing growth.

The first challenge is one of developing terms that accurately describe these places and concisely capture the nature of their conditions. In April 2011, the American Assembly of Columbia University, in collaboration with the Center for Community Progress and the Center for Sustainable Urban Development of Columbia University's Earth Institute, sought to address these cities, their unique assets, and their profound structural challenges. The Assembly chose to identify cities

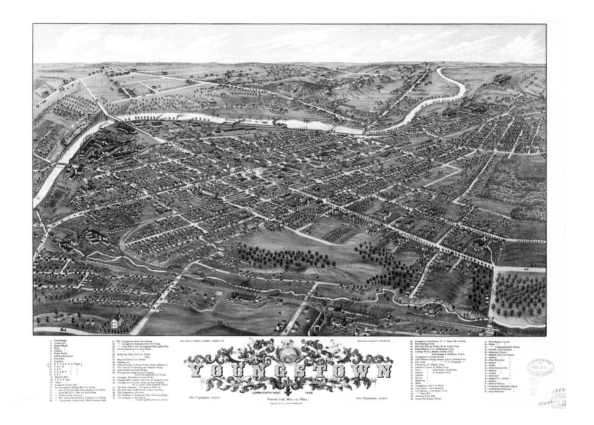

Fig. 1. 1882 aerial view
of Youngstown

that are experiencing severe, persistent population loss as "legacy cities," believing that this term best describes both the assets they have inherited from the industrial era of the nineteenth and twentieth centuries and the liabilities that weigh them down as they attempt to emerge healthy and competitive in the more complex global economy of the twenty-first century.

Youngstown, Ohio, was an early innovator in the effort to deal honestly and creatively with the consequences of deindustrialization and prolonged depopulation. Youngstown was one of the first American cities to deindustrialize and emerged in the early years of the twenty-first century as a leader among the nation's historically industrial communities. This chapter describes the community's effort to develop and implement a civic vision and some of the lessons learned as a consequence.

Steel City, USA

Youngstown is a mid-sized city located midway between Pittsburgh and Cleveland in the center of a cluster of industrial communities known

for over a century as the Steel Belt and in the past four decades as
the Rust Belt (fig. 1). Over the course of 150 years, it became the center
of a continuous chain of steel mill towns that lined 30 miles of the
Mahoning Valley. "Thirty mills in thirty miles" was for many years
the valley's tag line. At its peak, the valley was the nation's third-largest
producer of iron and steel and became known as "America's Ruhr
Valley." Today, Youngstown remains the largest and best-known city
in a bistate metropolitan area of approximately 600,000.

Youngstown's growth as a major center of the nation's iron and steel
industry began in 1803 when James and Daniel Heaton built the first
ballast furnace. The ready availability of coal, water, and old-growth
forests from which to make charcoal combined with the steady expansion of the region's transportation infrastructure—first canals and later
railroads—led to the development of an iron industry in the valley.
The beginning of the twentieth century saw the emergence of the
American steel industry. With the conversion from iron (which required
skilled craftsmen) to steel (which required a larger and generally less-
skilled labor force), Youngstown and its neighboring communities
began to attract large numbers of immigrants from Europe and later the
American South to fill an ever-growing number of jobs. With the surge
of immigrants came the development of working-class neighborhoods
on the hills and in the valleys within walking distance of the "works."

Youngstown's population surged, growing from 8,000 residents in 1870
to 15,000 just ten years later. It doubled again in 1890 to 33,000 and
again in 1910 to 79,000. By 1930 Youngstown reached an all-time peak
population of 170,000. The city's population declined modestly during
the Great Depression to 168,000 and remained at approximately that
level for the next thirty years. With the development of new neighborhoods in the adjacent suburbs and the creation of the regional freeway
network, those who could leave the city began to do so. By 1970—the
last census before the collapse of the steel industry—Youngstown had
lost 16 percent of its population, declining to 140,000. By 1980, the city
had lost another 17 percent of its population and declined to 115,000;
by 1990 another 17 percent to 95,787; and by 2000 14.4 percent to
82,026. The 2010 census determined that the city's population was
69,982—a further loss of 18.3 percent. The city now has 9,000 fewer
people than it had one hundred years ago.

The story of postindustrial Youngstown began abruptly on Black
Monday, September 19, 1977. On that day, the LTV Corporation—

Fig. 2. Demolition of the
Ohio Steel Works

the new owners of the Youngstown Iron Sheet and Tube Company—
shuttered its Campbell Works and announced that it would close most
of its remaining operations in the valley by the end of that week. As a
result of that one action, five thousand employees lost their jobs perma-
nently and a riptide of deindustrialization soon followed. Within two
years, U.S. Steel abandoned the valley, and the network of firms that
supported the steel industry began, one by one, to downsize, move,
or go out of business (fig. 2).

In the years following Black Monday, the communities that had housed
the valley's prosperous unionized industrial work force began to empty
out. Throughout the city, whole neighborhoods emptied out as families
left the city in search of work in more prosperous places. Downtown
Youngstown, long the valley's most significant retail center, collapsed.
By 2000, once teeming sidewalks were lined with empty storefronts
and commercial buildings sprouting trees through collapsed roofs.

The economic impact on the city was likewise devastating. In the
wake of Black Monday and the wave of plant closings that followed,
Youngstown lost 40 percent of its tax base; experienced unemployment levels that approached 25 percent; saw dramatic increases in
personal bankruptcy, housing abandonment, divorce, and domestic
violence; and became a national symbol of America's growing Rust Belt.
Youngstown experienced devastation that is on the scale that New
Orleans suffered following Hurricane Katrina, but in slow motion,
and over the course of decades, not days.

Shrinking by Design: Youngstown 2010 and the Search for a New Narrative

For over a century, Youngstown identified itself with the iron and steel industry and saw its success only in terms of the production of ferrous metals. Efforts to diversify the economy were dismissed: the good times were just too good to risk changing a winning formula. Like the much larger city of Detroit, which as the "Motor City" put all of its chips on the manufacturing of motor vehicles, Youngstown prospered for decades as an industrial monoculture—in contemporary terms, an "industrial cluster." When the steel industry collapsed in Youngstown and throughout the Mahoning Valley, the firms that supported it collapsed as well, multiplying the economic impact on the local economy.

Because it had clung tenaciously to its civic identity as "Steel City, USA," Youngstown's corporate community, political leadership, and citizenry were poorly equipped to adjust to the harsh reality that the city would no longer produce steel or experience the prosperity that came with it. The community fought for almost a decade to bring the steel industry back through employee ownership of the closed mills. They enlisted Ohio senator Howard Metzenbaum in a successful effort to pass national plant-closing legislation that would provide some measure of protection to workers the next time a company decided to shut its factory forever. But their effort ultimately failed, only deepening the sense of hopelessness and despair.

As the decade of the 1980s passed, Youngstown saw its civic identity change from "Steel City" to "Mob City," as organized crime and political corruption grabbed the local headlines and stole the imagination of the national media. During these years, Youngstown's leadership pursued a series of "silver bullet" projects that they promised would bring prosperity back to the valley. Local officials and business leaders repeatedly promised that the valley would soon see factories producing blimps, airplanes, and Avanti sports cars; a new U.S. Department of Defense payroll center; a new cargo hub at the regional airport; and an indoor motor car track. In time the community learned that these promises were false. And with every hope raised and dashed, the community's despair and cynicism grew.

Pursuing Civic Alignment

Eventually a new civic consciousness appeared, leading ultimately to a renewed sense of hope and a new plan for the future, Youngstown 2010. This plan was the result of a unique partnership between the city of Youngstown and Youngstown State University. This collaboration commenced in 2002 when Mayor George McKelvey and President David Sweet met and agreed to co-convene a community planning process. They set a target date of 2010—some eight years in the future—in the belief that the community would respond best to the planning process if it was undertaken with a tight time horizon that conveyed a sense of urgency.

Youngstown began its pursuit of civic alignment serendipitously and somewhat modestly in 1999. That year the Charles Stewart Mott Foundation of Flint, Michigan, contracted with Richard C. Harwood, a community engagement consultant, to benchmark Flint with two other similarly sized cities, Youngstown and Chattanooga, Tennessee. Harwood and his organization (then known as the Harwood Group and now known as the Harwood Institute) came to Youngstown, identified thirty-five community leaders, invited them to participate in "living room conversations," and evaluated the results using his proprietary scale of civic attitudes, the "Five Stages of Community Life."

Harwood subsequently issued a report, *Waiting for the Future: Creating New Possibilities for Youngstown.* The group observed that while Youngstown had many assets with which to build a new and more promising future, its civic leadership was unable to empower itself to move forward. "Indeed, Youngstown seems to be waiting for an intervention of some sort to help pull everyone together and push ahead," Harwood reported. "People define intervention differently—an infusion of government money, a community plan, a strong leader. But there is a sense that the city is just waiting."[2]

Youngstown's civic structure, in so many words, was still locked into the hierarchical and authoritarian decision-making model of the industrial city. Its people were waiting for "the boss"—the mill owner, the foreman, the mayor, the congressman—to tell them what to do rather than taking initiative on their own behalf. Twenty years had passed since the mills closed and the industrial hierarchies disappeared, and yet the people of Youngstown were acting as though the social hierarchies they created still existed.

Harwood's report had a profound and lasting impact on the city's leadership. It galvanized the Youngstown City Council to set aside money to update the city's decades-old general plan. It encouraged the Youngstown State University (YSU) board of trustees to replace a retiring president with someone who would be a civic coalition builder. And it set the stage for the launch of Youngstown 2010, a community planning process that finally altered the city's trajectory.

A year after Harwood issued his report, the trustees of YSU selected Dr. David C. Sweet, then dean of the Maxine Goodman Levin College of Urban Affairs at Cleveland State University, as their new president. Upon assuming office, Sweet immediately began to build partnerships and coalitions that, over time, helped Youngstown to achieve a better alignment of its assets and its actors. Upon learning of the city's desire to update its general plan, Sweet proposed to Mayor George McKelvey a unique city-university collaboration. The two agreed to co-convene and jointly staff the planning process. The mayor appointed Jay Williams, then the director of the city's Community Development Agency (and now the city's mayor), as the city lead, and Sweet invited the author to head the university team. Sweet agreed to suspend pending action on the development of a new university master plan until the city planning process was further along.

The city-university planning team began by engaging an outside urban planning consultant, Urban Strategies of Toronto, Canada, to assist in the first phase of the work—the "vision" phase. The intent of this phase was to produce "an agreed-upon set of community goals and a description of the changes needed to achieve these goals."[3] The planning process began by building on the Harwood methodology and engaging over two hundred civic leaders, representing a broad cross section of the community, in focus groups designed to elicit the vision's major themes.

Coming to Accept Hard Truths
The team received over six hundred comments and recommendations from the focus group series. Based on their findings, the team identified several broad themes with which to frame a new community vision and consolidated their recommendations into four "thematic pillars":

Acceptance: Youngstown needs to accept the fact that it is no longer a big city and strive to be a model of a sustainable mid-sized city. In essence, the community needs to accept the reality of decades of depopulation and define a civic identity that replaces the emphasis on number of people in the city with quality of life for those who remained.

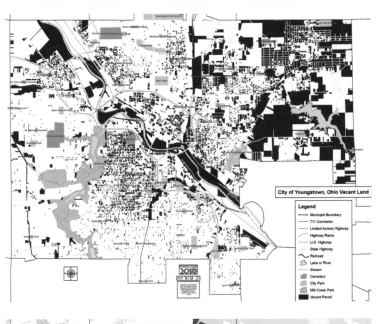

Fig. 3. Map of vacant parcels

Fig. 4. Map of current land use

Opposite: Fig. 5. Map of
projected land use

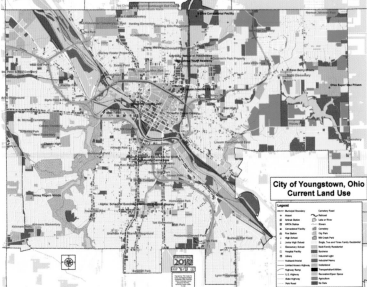

Alignment: Youngstown needs to realign itself to compete in new
regional and global economies. The community should look for
economic opportunity beyond the Mahoning Valley and recognize
the challenges and opportunities that exist on larger playing fields.

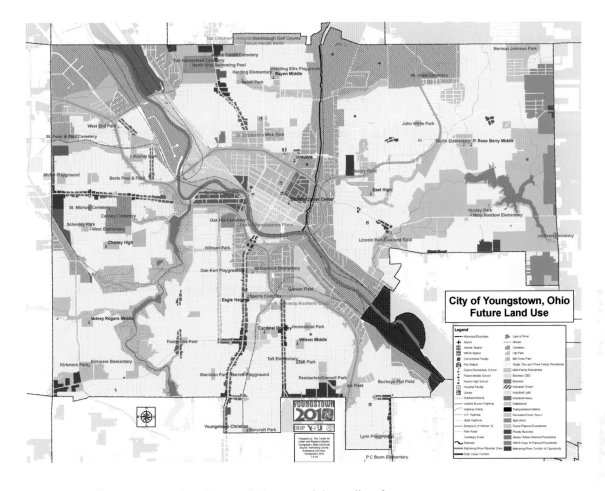

Improvement: Youngstown needs to focus on its image and the quality of life in its neighborhoods. On the one hand, the community should recognize the corrosive nature of the negative press that the city had received for many years and make a concerted effort to reframe its image. On the other hand, the city needs to focus on implementing tangible changes that will make Youngstown a better place to live and work.

Action: Youngstown needs to take action. Rather than being content with a new plan, the community needs to take specific steps to implement its vision and celebrate inclusively when it succeeds in accomplishing these steps.

The city-university-consultant team presented the proposed vision to the community at a public meeting on a snowy Sunday evening in late December 2002. That meeting saw the first indications that a new civic alignment was emerging in Youngstown. Rather than a small audience composed of the "usual suspects" who routinely attend public planning meetings, over 1,400 citizens of Youngstown and the Mahoning Valley came out to listen, learn, and share their thoughts. Rather than expressing skepticism, cynicism, and hostility, the majority of the speakers shared their aspirations and expectations for the future and expressed support of the effort to craft a new city plan. The fact that over one hundred citizens volunteered that night to work on the plan astounded team members long accustomed to widespread indifference to participating in long-range planning processes.

The team noted that the community appeared ready to accept the reality of being a smaller-sized city and to embrace a new narrative that focused on sustainability and quality of life rather than on population size. They saw the absence of both the angry nostalgia for Youngstown's past and the tendency to blame others for the collapse of the steel industry. Instead, they heard a cautious optimism, a willingness to consider new ideas, and a desire to move forward as a community. While two years of community meetings would take place before the city came forward with the Youngstown 2010 Plan, the core themes articulated that night remained the basic framework of the city's new narrative.

Taking Action

After presenting the vision to the Youngstown City Council for its endorsement, the planning team convened community meetings, task forces, and citizen advisory groups and spent the next two years developing a new action-oriented plan to replace the existing city plan, first adopted in the 1950s and amended twenty years later (figs. 3–5). Encouraged by the enthusiasm of the citizens who volunteered to help and aware of the amount of work that had to be accomplished with a limited staff, the team decided to fully engage the volunteers in updating the city's plan. The team clustered the city's thirty-one distinct neighborhoods into eleven "neighborhood planning districts" and organized the staff and volunteers into six working groups. Staff and volunteers developed the content for community meetings in each of the groups. Over 160 volunteers participated in the following working groups during 2003 and early 2004:

Fix Up, Cleanup, and Beautification: This group trained forty volunteers to carry out a visual survey of buildings, vacant properties, and sidewalk conditions. The group surveyed every parcel in the city, and the university's geographic information system (GIS) team mapped and analyzed the results. The team then used the maps at the eleven neighborhood district meetings to show attendees the conditions existing in their community.

Housing for Emerging Markets: This group analyzed census information as well as the visual survey and made recommendations regarding the opportunities for new housing types to meet the city's changing demography. The group presented their findings at the neighborhood meetings in order to refine their recommendations.

Enjoying Our Natural Amenities: This group made recommendations regarding how best to utilize the city's considerable park and recreational amenities in a fiscal environment of reduced municipal resources. They identified vacant land suitable for future park expansion and recommended creating a network of bike routes and pedestrian trails that would connect these resources to each other and to the adjacent neighborhoods.

Youngstown's New Economy: This group analyzed the city economy in relation to the regional economy and identified the need to conduct a more detailed analysis of commercial centers and downtown economic functions using a team of professional consultants.

New Image for Youngstown: This group collaborated with a local marketing firm that volunteered its staff to develop a coordinated marketing program for the Youngstown 2010 planning process. The campaign augmented the customary newspaper articles and public service announcements with billboards, bumper stickers, an informational brochure, and an integrated effort to "brand" major city and university projects as Youngstown 2010 initiatives. The group collaborated with the local PBS affiliate to air quarterly "Reports to the People" during the two-year planning process.

Neighborhood-Based Planning: This group assisted the city-university team in outreach to each of the city's communities and in conducting the eleven neighborhood cluster meetings. It distributed the informational brochure developed by the New Image for Youngstown group to businesses, neighborhood organizations, and residents to inform them about their neighborhood meetings.

The city-university team used the input from the working groups and over eight hundred participants in neighborhood meetings to generate a draft land-use plan. This plan was made available for public review at the city's libraries and at other convenient locations. The team presented the draft plan to over 1,300 members of the public (not including the public television–viewing audience) at Stambaugh Auditorium on January 27, 2005. Enthusiasm for the planning process was evidenced not just by the size of the audience that night but also by the level of civic engagement in the multiyear planning process: in all over five thousand people participated directly in crafting the plan. Broad public support for the 2010 plan was further evidenced by the fact that Youngstown voters subsequently passed—by 74 percent—a charter amendment requiring that the city update its plan every decade.

"Taking Action" was not limited to adopting a new city plan. Following the approval of the Youngstown 2010 Plan, YSU began to develop its own master plan. Completed in 2008, the Centennial Campus Master Plan addressed on-campus facility needs and identified opportunities in the off-campus districts within a half of a mile of the campus boundaries. Both the university and the city saw these walk-to neighborhoods as the most promising locations for new housing and retail to serve the campus population. At the same time, YSU and the Youngstown Symphony collaborated on the expansion of a downtown recital hall for joint use. The university commenced planning for a new business school that would extend its campus southward toward downtown, and the city assisted the university in assembling the site and extending the downtown street grid northward to serve it.

As the Youngstown 2010 Plan was being completed, the city began to develop a long-delayed project to construct a new 5,000-seat arena in downtown Youngstown. Private developers and nonprofit institutions responded to opportunities identified by the plan. Developers built several hundred apartment units to meet the needs of university students and downtown workers, and the Youngstown Business Incubator constructed a new downtown office building to accommodate its growing portfolio of businesses. The Mahoning Valley Historical Society followed suit, deciding to locate its Historical Center in the adjacent Harry Burt/Ross Radio Building, an historic building known as the site where Good Humor Ice Cream was invented and first sold. More recently, the Youngstown Children's Museum completed "Oh Wow," a new state-of-the-art facility on Federal Square, in the heart of downtown Youngstown.

Within the limits of its severely constrained municipal budget, the city moved to address the challenges posed by continued abandonment in its neighborhoods. City teams, working with neighborhood institutions and citizens, targeted demolition funds to remove abandoned buildings on its major arterial roadways and from other prominent sites. By doing so, the city improved the curb appeal of the adjacent neighborhoods. At the same time, it removed the visual evidence of depopulation and replaced empty buildings with landscaped sites. The city adopted a program of rental inspection and landlord registration to improve the quality of the city's stock of rental properties. It collaborated with Mahoning County to establish Lien Forward, a countywide land bank capable of assembling, enhancing, and marketing tax-delinquent properties. Finally, the city received funding from the state of Ohio to update its existing zoning code and tailor it to address the unique needs of a city that has lost over half of its population and has little prospect of significant redevelopment of the residential and commercial property left behind.

The years since the Youngstown City Council formally adopted the Youngstown 2010 Plan have seen an unprecedented level of innovation and collaboration. The economic shocks that befell the nation in the fall of 2008 and the subprime-loan disaster that crippled the housing market further burdened Youngstown with unmarketable inventory. Yet the community developed several new nonprofit organizations to coalesce resources to address persistent community development challenges. Youngstown's downtown beautification committee merged with the city's small but dedicated historic preservation community to form CityScape, a new organization dedicated to improving the visual quality of the city and preserving its remaining historical assets. The local Raymond John Wean Foundation established the Mahoning Valley Organizing Collaborative to carry out neighborhood organizing in Youngstown and Warren and to spur neighborhood action. The Wean Foundation also created the Youngstown Neighborhood Development Corporation to address pressing needs in Youngstown neighborhoods. This organization collaborates with existing neighborhood associations and targets several neighborhoods that appear to have long-term prospects of surviving in the face of continued residential abandonment.

America's Legacy Cities: New Narratives for Old Places
Youngstown has the distinction of being among the first American industrial cities to deindustrialize. Now the city has achieved the distinction of being the first American industrial city to acknowledge as a matter

of public policy and popular endorsement that it is—and for the foreseeable future will remain—a city that is smaller than it was during the height of the industrial era. By abandoning population size as its principal metric of success, the Youngstown community has opened a continuing dialogue about what sort of city it should strive to become. As a consequence, it has begun to develop the coherent political language that enables citizens and their elected officials to discuss openly the consequences of having a smaller population and the choices facing the community as it strives to be a sustainable mid-sized city.

Few other legacy cities have been able to have a civil discourse about their future as a place with a smaller population. Most local elected officials prefer to deny the long-term and pernicious nature of the abandonment of their city and continue to offer platitudes and big projects in an attempt to convince a skeptical public that the good times will someday return.

Youngstown, within its constrained resources, has pioneered the effort to understand the dynamics of shrinking cities and has collaborated with organizations such as Greater Ohio, a state affiliate of the Brookings Institution, and the Center for Community Progress to serve as a laboratory for testing different ways to meet the challenges it and many other Great Lakes industrial communities face.

The attention that Youngstown continues to receive from the media and academic communities and from the leaders of other cities, both in the United States and abroad, is evidence that Youngstown is not alone in searching for ways to manage a profound economic transformation. Legacy cities—and other communities faced with managing unprecedented change—can use the lessons that Youngstown has learned to design and implement practical strategies for economic transformation. These include:

Start Small and Build Consensus through Structured Civic Conversations: Legacy cities need to encourage broad discussions that enable its citizens to identify and articulate a new civic vision—a meaningful future that draws on a community's remaining assets. Youngstown's planning team found that by starting with small groups of community leaders and listening actively, it could develop a broad consensus about the issues facing the community. As word of these civic conversations spread, more people chose to participate. Focused civic conversations take time to develop but enable citizens to connect with each other in deeper, more meaningful ways.

Develop New Narratives: Legacy cities need to define new narratives that build on their strengths and project an authentic and positive view of the next generation. Youngstown's decision to redefine itself as a "sustainable mid-sized city" has spurred community-wide actions directed at making Youngstown a greener, more livable and sustainable community:

> The community initiated an annual "Gray to Green Festival," started a weekly farmers market and created a Mahoning Valley Food Council to address "food deserts" and promote community-supported agriculture.

> The university's board of trustees required that the new Williamson College of Business Administration be built to LEED Gold standard and appropriated the funds needed to reach that goal.

> The university's STEM (Science, Technology, Engineering and Mathematics) College convenes an annual Advanced Energy conference and actively pursues research in solar and wind technology.

> The Youngstown Neighborhood Development Corporation (YNDC) combines neighborhood organizing, targeted demolition of abandoned houses, and community gardening to reestablish safe, attractive, walkable communities in three parkside neighborhoods: Idora Park, Crandall Park, and Lincoln Park. Two other parkside neighborhoods (Wick Park and Rocky Ridge) have learned from the YNDC's experiences and are applying these lessons to their own communities.

> The city and the Youngstown Regional Chamber of Commerce have, at long last, embraced historic preservation and have collaborated to support the adaptive reuse of several long-abandoned historic office buildings in downtown Youngstown.

> The voters of Mahoning County voted to support a county-wide levy enabling the Western Reserve Transit Authority to restore and expand bus service throughout the city, improve service to the university and other major employers, and extend service to the adjacent city of Warren.

Be Honest with Yourself: Communities, like people, need to be honest with themselves about the challenges they face so they can address them successfully. The Youngstown community found that when it publicly acknowledged that it was—and would likely remain—a demographically smaller community, it gave up wishful thinking. This acceptance liberated the community leadership to think in new ways. Leaders became free to make hard choices about demolishing blighted buildings, targeting limited incentive funds, and fallowing long-abandoned neighborhoods.

Be Coherent and Visualize Your Future(s): Economic transformation is bewilderingly complex. Visualizations help make sense of these changes and explore our options. Legacy cities need to use maps, videos, simulation, social media, and other tools to orient people to where they stand and where they are going. Youngstown took advantage of YSU's GIS capacity to develop visual tools that helped its citizens understand the patterns of disinvestment and identify the physical assets upon which to build a new future. It actively used the local PBS affiliate to engage the entire Mahoning Valley in a three-year discussion about Youngstown's future.

Act Strategically by Doing Things That Matter: Legacy cities need to see "planning" and "doing" as coincident and mutually supportive activities. Communities, like individuals, gain alignment through planning and gain insight from action. The Youngstown community has pursued "strategic doing," a disciplined and agile approach to learning what works. It has identified projects that aligned with its vision and focused limited community resources on carrying them out. Based on its experience, the community continues to refine and focus its vision.

Celebrate Successes Inclusively: Too often communities portray their successes as the work of an individual or small group rather than the work of many hands. Leaders of legacy cities need to learn to say "thank you" and to share credit for projects that advance the common good. Celebrating a successfully completed project as a community success story establishes a positive narrative that over time replaces the vicious cycle of hopelessness and decline with a virtuous cycle of hopefulness and reinvestment. Youngstown learned to share credit by portraying individual projects as contributing to the implementation of the Youngstown 2010 Vision and Plan. Its public officials routinely share credit for high-profile projects, while community leaders tie individual projects to the broader civic narrative that the plan and process first articulated.

The challenge ahead for legacy cities of the Great Lakes region is managing transformation, not growth. This requires that planners and public officials develop a common language with which to discuss the challenges faced by these cities and together chart the way forward. This language must redefine what the word "success" means for cities that have lost significant population and have no realistic possibility of returning to their former size.

By admitting that it is—and will remain—a smaller city than it was during the industrial era, Youngstown has taken a critical first step in developing a language with which to discuss a new future free of civic expectation that it strive to once again be "Steel City, USA." It has developed and strengthened its leadership skills and is now better able than in prior decades to collaborate, innovate, act, and celebrate its common successes. As a more agile and self-confident city, Youngstown is better able to respond to emerging economic opportunities, learn from its experiences, and tell its story to the world.

Much remains to be done—both in Youngstown and in other Great Lakes legacy cities—to address the impact of chronic disinvestment in the nation's industrial cities and the attendant loss of population and economic strength. Youngstown's story is a story shared by many of the nation's legacy cities. As such, it offers lessons—both hopeful and cautionary—to all those who live in, work in, and care about these communities.

---

1   As cited by Justin B. Hollander et al., "Planning Shrinking Cities," *Progress in Planning* 72, no. 4 (2009), 223–32.

2   Harwood Group, *Waiting for the Future: Creating New Possibilities for Youngstown* (Bethesda, Md.: Harwood Group, 1999), 20.

3   Thomas A. Finnerty, Jr., *Youngstown 2010 Citywide Plan* (Youngstown, Ohio: City of Youngstown, 2005), 135.

Retrench-
ment,
Revitalization,
or the
Right to the
City?:
Four Theses
Don
Mitchell

Are we who live in deindustrialized Rust Belt cities of the American
Northeast somehow "formerly urban"? In the provocation that follows,
I argue that any answer in the affirmative is tantamount to conceding
loss even before the battle has begun. Instead, I argue, we need to more
fully embrace—and advance—the promise of the urban, and that the
way to do so is to take seriously and begin to organize around a positive right to the city, a right that must sit at the heart of any socially just
urban future, not only here, but globally.

*The problem confronting us is not decline but active disinvestment—
and class-based reinvestment.*

Uneven and unequal development is a capitalist imperative.[1] Capitalism
simply cannot "lift all boats." As Marx made so clear, a relative,
progressive immiseration must sit at the heart of capitalist social relations, but so too must it take a geographical form.[2] Joseph Schumpeter
called the combined economic, social, and geographical processes
at work "creative destruction," and whether creative or not, such
forces are certainly destructive to the people who are subject to them.[3]
Hard-won skills become obsolete overnight, whole industries are wiped
from the face of the earth, cities and neighborhoods are turned into
ghost towns or violent dystopias.

For example, when the steel mills closed in Johnstown, Pennsylvania,
in the early 1980s, and official employment rates exceeded 25 percent,
the city not only faced a staggering fiscal crisis but also saw rates of
domestic violence quickly rise to the highest levels in the state. The
active *un*-development of Johnstown, a process whose planning dated
back to the early 1960s (if not earlier), did not mark the end of "development." Rather, it marked its geographical relocation—in this case to
Utah, South Korea, Brazil, and other outposts of the far-flung Bethlehem
Steel empire—as the managers of the capital that was steel production in Johnstown sought new low-wage, minimally regulated frontiers.
What was at work was an active devaluation of both the labor and the
fixed capital of Johnstown—the built landscape of homes, stores, and
infrastructure as well as the machinery and so forth that this landscape
supported—a devaluation that extended from the heart of downtown out
into the neighborhoods, not leaving unscathed even the wealthier hill-
top enclaves and suburban acres of the managerial classes.[4]

Crisis sharpens these processes, and places like Johnstown felt their
immiseration rapidly and seemingly irrevocably deepen during the

crises of the 1970s and 1980s that ushered in the era of so-called deindustrialization.[5] Wages fell, and the value of labor power was significantly undermined. "Devaluation of productive capital in the course of crisis and the rapid expansion that follows," Neil Smith argues, "are place-specific."[6] That is, there is no reason that the expansion of productive capacity that follows economic crises will happen where that capacity had just years or months earlier been so thoroughly devalued. To Smith's point about productive capital, we could also add the capital fixed in the infrastructure of social reproduction—houses, stores, parks, whole neighborhoods—and thus a destruction of the value of labor power, since its value is already defined (like all other commodities) as the sum of the values that go into its production but also the sum of the values necessary for its *reproduction*. Such sums (for its production and its reproduction) possess in the case of labor power what Marx called a "historical and moral element," which is to say that the value of labor power is an achievement of social struggle: every upward push on wages is a hard-won victory that also, perhaps, increases laborers' share of the social product at the expense of the capitalists' share; every downward shove on wages is a victory for capital (if a contradictory one, since it also undermines consumer markets).[7] Everyday *un*-development, or creative destruction, abetted by periodic crises is the place-specific means by which the equation of surplus-value extraction is reset on terms once again more favorable to capital. The problem, then, confronting "shrinking cities" like Johnstown, Detroit, Syracuse, Buffalo, or Youngstown is not one of "decline," as it is often described, but rather one of active, planned, and systematically *necessary* disinvestment.

Struggles over un-development—deindustrialization has certainly been resisted—are not only interclass struggles but also intra-class struggles.[8] Much capital is locally rooted. The capital fixed in small metalwork shops; in the myriad services necessary for place-based production and reproduction; in stores, bars, and restaurants; in newspapers and other media infrastructure; and in the goods of collective consumption, like sewers and roadways, often built and maintained by local firms, cannot get up and leave with quite the same alacrity as the finance capital that sloshes through the accounts of firms whose scale extends more region-ally, nationally, or globally. Not all capital is—or can be—"footloose."[9] As is well known, then, locally rooted factions of capital typically form the nucleus of locally based "growth-machines" dedicated to attracting new mobile capital so that locally implanted investments will be secured.[10] The effects of growth-machine practices and politics are well studied and well known, the most important of which is that places are thrown into vicious competition with each other in a seemingly zero-sum game to attract new capital, perhaps at any cost.[11] Another effect can only be described as desperation: a seemingly uncontrollable impulse to follow every development and marketing fad trumpeted by the latest "charismatic economic-development troubadour," from the scramble in the 1990s for aquariums, new old-fashioned baseball stadiums, neotraditional "new urbanist" neighborhoods, and a post-modern Michael Graves signature building, to the clamor in the 2000s for the creative class, sidewalk dining, and Gehry bent-metal buildings—all in an attempt to make one's city distinctive in exactly the same way as every other city, and thereby attract the same footloose capital everyone else is bidding for, *and* the creative souls in whose pockets it seems to rest.[12]

Reinvestment then takes on a decided class character, with particular official focus trained on gentrifying specific sections of town—usually old warehouse areas immediately adjacent to downtown—creating living spaces and playgrounds for the elite who hardly need them. This can have positive effects, no doubt: if urban space has undergone some kind of "pacification by cappuccino," at least now there is cappuccino.[13] But we should not kid ourselves about spillover effects. In most smallish northeastern cities, it is not a far walk from gentrified warehouses and brewpubs to empty former main street shopping districts, abandoned semi-industrial districts, and class- and race-segregated housing ghettos, though it is usually a walk across a stark and obvious line.[14] Nor should we kid ourselves about what happens when neighborhood development—especially development in poor neighborhoods—is left to the good works (and they are good works) of charitable and nonprofit organizations whose very ability to do their work is a function of the largess of others (and, of course, skill in beating out their competitors in other neighbor-hoods or other cities for dwindling pots of grant dollars). Uneven development operates at every scale.

The typically prescribed responses, retrenchment and reinvestment, do not address the root of the problem.

Against the bleak picture I have just painted, some important coun-terstrategies have arisen, the most significant of which, perhaps, is a wholesale geographical retrenchment: the shrinking cities movement. There is much of interest here, and much to be lauded. The gutsiness that accompanied the decision of Youngstown, Ohio, not to grow but to better plan its own shrinkage should not be underestimated.[15] For all manner of environmental, social, political, and economic reasons, this is an important, even revolutionary move. But it is also a limited one. At its heart, the shrinking cities movement defines a *reinvestment—* and fiscal—strategy, only now targeting a smaller footprint, and seeking out the funds that will allow for the mothballing or ripping out of infrastructure, the demolishing of houses, and so forth. It is designed to turn a totally de-developed, actively disinvested, devalued city into a manageable, more compact, more "livable" town. But as John Russo and James Rhodes of Youngstown State University's Center for Working-Class Studies have recently pointed out, Youngstown's success in attracting reinvestment downtown (as per its shrinking cities plan) has come at the cost of "ignor[ing] the city's real problems: high unemployment, poverty, continued high crime rates, and the deterioration of Youngstown's neighborhoods."[16] The last of these problems—the deterioration of the neighborhoods—is Russo and Rhodes's primary concern, and the story they tell is depressing in the extreme. The standard of living for most Youngstowners has continued to decrease, they show, and with that local businesses continue to go belly up, even as new restaurants and boutiques open downtown. There are now more renters than homeowners in what used to be called the "City of Homes," and absentee landlordism is a growing problem.

"Shrinking Youngstown," write Russo and Rhodes, "has proven difficult to enact; long-time responsible residents of deteriorating neighborhoods often do not want to move. They want more and better services to stabilize their neighborhoods. Without a workable plan and stronger leadership, Youngstown's shrinkage has been uneven, and it's hard to see significant change." Indeed, the grass-roots "Mahoning Valley Organizing Collaborative and its many neighborhood associations have become the de facto community planning agency" in Youngstown, and this is potentially quite a good thing. But, as Russo and Rhodes go on to note, "neither the Mayor nor county government leaders regularly attend community meetings." The upshot has been what they call a "tale of two cities." Youngstown, they write:

> is an increasingly divided city. On the one hand, we can see Youngstown's Renaissance in the thriving restaurants downtown, the success of the business incubator, and the growth of the university. But the rest of the city is merely surviving. Even as successful neighborhood groups plant gardens and keep blockwatches going, for too many local residents, having safe housing and healthy food is a daily effort, a struggle made all the more challenging amid fear

of being shot or robbed. That is why the most pressing issue for
Youngstown and the Mahoning Valley is the economic stabilization
of its neighborhoods. We need to improve the standard of living in
these neighborhoods.[17]

Indeed. But listen to what Russo and Rhodes say next. "Imagine,"
they write, "what could happen if the creative, educated, technically
sophisticated, and energetic young professionals who are advocating
downtown redevelopment and our government officials made neighborhood revitalization a priority." There's the problem. It names what
might be a necessary, if not even close to sufficient, solution to what
is surely the wrong problem. It suggests the problem is a problem of
investment as such, rather than the basis upon which investment operates. Yes, as Russo and Rhodes argue, "They [the creative types and
the government officials] must understand that changing the image of
Youngstown will not save the city unless the material conditions of most
residents improve." That's absolutely true. But such an improvement—
at least anything like a *lasting* improvement—is chimerical just so long
as improving material conditions is based on a strategy of investment
in exchange value.

*Cities built around exchange value can do nothing to address uneven
and unequal development, though they may occasionally be able to ride
its bow wave.*

For all that is right in Russo and Rhode's argument, what's missing is
a critique of the exchange-value foundation of contemporary efforts
to remake shrinking or disinvested cities. The goal is to protect and
enhance what exchange value might remain in old buildings and infrastructure or in land, or to produce new exchange values that can be
leveraged and traded on the market. Downtown and even neighborhood revitalization is predicated first and foremost on improving the
economic value of land; the sign of success is increased property values.
But as the very idea of shrinking cities makes so clear, such a goal
does nothing to address the underlying problems of uneven development. Indeed, shrinking the city is predicated on uneven development:
some neighborhoods or districts are wiped clean precisely so that the
exchange values in others may be enhanced. Or perhaps it is more
accurate to say, as David Harvey did long ago, that the primary purpose
for producing use-values is to advance capitalist accumulation.
"Capital represents itself in the form of a physical landscape created in
its own image," Harvey argued, "created as use-values to enhance the

progressive accumulation of capital."[18] When such use-values are no longer useful, not to people, but to the project of capital accumulation, they must be destroyed. As Harvey continued:

Activists from Picture the Homeless demonstrating for the "right to the city"

> Capitalist development has to negotiate a knife-edge path between preserving the exchange values of past capital investment in the built environment and destroying the value of those investments in order to open up fresh room for accumulation. Under capitalism there is then a perpetual struggle in which capital builds up a physical landscape appropriate to its own condition at a particular moment in time only to have to destroy it, usually in the course of a crisis, at a subsequent point in time. The temporal and geographical ebb and flow of investment in the built environment can be understood only in terms of such a process.[19]

Only to the degree that organizations like the Mahoning Valley Organizing Collaborative face this fact head-on will there be any chance that the problems of continuing neighborhood disinvestment that Russo and Rhodes detail will be anything other than inevitable. Without accepting and addressing this fact, some neighborhoods, some districts might prosper, but we cannot hope to make a city (or a region) for all its people. We must, in other words, question directly just how retrenchment and revitalization are currently based in a zero-sum game of value rooted in exchange and begin to find ways to make it otherwise.[20]

We need to find ways, as many are doing, both to root our struggles more firmly in what might be called the social (as opposed to economic) use-value of property, buildings, and infrastructure, and to better theorize why doing so is so incredibly necessary—why retrenchment and reinvestment, as they are typically imagined, are simply not sufficient for the problems that face us.

Our focus needs to be organized around use-value, particularly under the banner of the right to the city.

Luckily, both the philosophical (or theoretical) and especially the political tools needed to effect such a reorientation toward use-value are in the process of being created. The vigorous movement under, and the multifaceted intellectual and practical debates over, the slogan "Right to the City" provide a new foundation for the thoroughgoing reconceptualization of redevelopment that will be necessary if we are to break free from the necessity of uneven development.[21]

The slogan "Right to the City" is most closely associated with the French sociologist, philosopher, and spatial theorist Henri Lefebvre.[22] In a series of writings, but especially in his short book *Le Droit à la Ville* (1968), written for the centennial of the publication of Marx's *Capital* (1867), Lefebvre sketched out an argument about the need to construct cities based not primarily in exchange and the accumulation of capital but in use, and especially what he called the right to participate in the making of the city.[23] Lefebvre saw the city as a work—an oeuvre—not a once-and-for-all thing, and the right to be central to that making was a primary right, one upon which other rights (for example, to speech or to housing) had to be predicated.

"The right to the city," Lefebvre argues, "manifests itself as a superior form of rights: right to freedom, to individualization in socialization, to habitat and to inhabit. The right to the *oeuvre*, to participation and *appropriation* (clearly distinct from the right to property), are implied in the right to the city."[24] In this sense, "the *right to the city* cannot be conceived of as a simple visiting right or as a return to traditional cities. It can only be formulated as a transformed and renewed *right to urban life*," which belongs "firstly [to] all those who *inhabit*" (not, then, firstly to the "creative class" or other outsiders we are constantly being sold as our saviors).[25] Lefebvre's language is redolent of a different way of thinking about cities than that proposed by political economy and planning focused primarily on economic development and the accumulation of capital.[26] He talks of

> rights-in-the-making which are not well-recognized, [but which] progressively become customary before being inscribed in formalized codes. They would change reality if they entered into social practice: right to work, to training and education, to health, housing, leisure, to life. Among these rights in the making features the right to the city (not to the ancient city, but to urban life, to renewed centrality, to places of encounter and exchange, to life rhythms and time uses, enabling the full and complete usage of these moments and places…). The proclamation and realization of urban life as the rule of use (of exchange and encounter disengaged from exchange value) insists on the mastery of the economic (of exchange value, the market, and commodities) and consequently is inscribed within the perspective of the revolution under the hegemony of the working class.[27]

In other words, if we were truly to take the right to the city seriously, it would necessitate a total revolution in the social relations that govern the contemporary political economy and social life itself. As I write, uprisings in Tunis, Cairo, Manama—and Madison (to say nothing of Dublin, Reykjavik, and university campuses across the U.K.)—make it clear that we live in revolutionary times. While the sort of global, urban, total revolution Lefebvre worked toward—a total one that establishes cities and the global political economy on new, more "commonistic" terms—might not yet be in the cards, there is no doubt that these revolutionary times are epoch making. Their roots are in the earlier, equally (counter-)revolutionary era of Thatcher and Reagan, which cemented into place so-called neoliberalism, sweeping away previous forms of social reproduction and replacing them with a new class settlement— the one today being globally contested—totally unfavorably to all but the precious, wealthy few.[28] But to interpret Lefebvre as only arguing for a total, rapid revolution is to miss his point. Rather, he is arguing that to the degree we understand the right to the city (in its myriad forms) to always be *rights in the making,* and especially to the degree we understand that such rights in the making are the DNA of the city as *oeuvre*, then to that degree, a total revolution in social relations and the re-founding of society around *usage*—the mastery of the economic— will necessarily follow. "The right to the city" names the struggle: what is to be struggled for and what quite possibly might result.

However, as Kafui Attoh persistently—and rightly—asks, just what kind of right is the right to the city?[29] At various times, Lefebvre defines it as (1) a right to inhabit and to habitat—(something like what legal philosopher Jeremy Waldron calls "second-generation" rights, such as the right to housing or to livelihood); (2) a right to life and to space (something akin to first-generation rights to bodily integrity, assembly, and speech, or political voice more broadly); and (3) a right to centrality, i.e., a right not to be marginal, and thus to fully participate in the making of urban society (something like third-generation or "cultural rights").[30] At times I have argued that the very value of the idea of a "right to the city" is its capaciousness—under such a broad banner, a whole range of social movements can find common cause—and that is true.[31] But it is also true, as Attoh insists, that we need to be clear just what we are fighting for so we can be aware of its limits.[32] If we limit the right to the city to the struggle for housing, as important and indispensible as that is, then we will miss the revolutionary potential of the struggle. If, by the same token, we struggle for a right to centrality—not just a voice in participatory planning, but a real struggle over hegemony in the planning and development process—if we seek primarily, as David Harvey has phrased the struggle, for the right to remake the city "after our heart's desire," then we risk missing out how the provision of housing might be a more important immediate issue, the un-fulfillment of which might make the right to centrality impossible.[33]

These sorts of debates are not just philosophical; they are deeply political and deeply pragmatic. They are right at the heart of the national and global Right to the City movements now forming. The NGO-centric UNESCO/UN-HABITAT-sponsored global Right to the City forums have at times been too narrowly focused on such questions as housing and clean water provision, rather than on housing or water provision within the context of an expansive right to be central in the *making* of the city. However, the exciting U.S.-based Right to the City Alliance—bringing together such diverse groups as the militant queer youth group FIERCE, and Picture the Homeless in New York City; City Life/Vida Urbana, which has been impressively effective in blocking evictions from foreclosed houses and apartments in Boston; Causa Justa/Just Cause in the Bay Area; the Olneyville Neighborhood Association in Providence; and the Miami Workers Center, to name only a few—has been insistent on a broad-based front that seeks to understand the interconnected nature of the different kinds of rights convened under the Right to the City banner and to engage in multifaceted campaigns that make it clear that the city must be a people's city (not capital's city), and that what urban commons there are left must be not just protected but expanded.[34]

Starkly pragmatic struggles—demanding more accountability from Providence's elected officials, especially around questions of economic development; fighting to maintain New York City's queer youths' access to a pier on the Hudson that has long been a safe space for them (as well as a home for some); or stopping evictions of renters when land-lords are foreclosed on in Boston, for example—are always couched in a fuller analysis of these struggles within the struggle for the larger right to the city. FIERCE has developed a strong coalition, for example, with renters and lower-income homeowners (often elderly) on the frontier of the gentrification of Hell's Kitchen, since the struggle to save their access to the pier is tied up closely with the struggle of poorer people to keep from getting pushed out of their homes by gentrification: the forces of development and "revitalization" at work in both instances are the same. More than that, though, these New York Right to the City struggles are consistently articulated through arguments about rights to be present, to centrality, to control over political-economic processes—all of which allow FIERCE to work productively (if not without tension) with organizations like Picture the Homeless that possess just as strong a sense of who the city *ought* to be for.

The point for all those struggling under the Right to the City banner is that city residents, especially less powerful residents, must be central to the making of any future city—whether revitalized, redeveloped, or retrenched. Innovation must arise from within the communities at the heart of any plans for development—or shrinkage. In this sense to think of Rust Belt cities as "formerly urban" (as some have begun to do) is, in fact, quite problematic. We should be thinking about how to make them *more* urban: *more* collective, *more* common, less a creature of the market or development fads. While it is true, as Lefebvre argued, that "urban life, urban society, in a word, the *urban* cannot go without a practico-material base, a morphology," it is even more true that the shaping of that morphology must arise from the needs, desires, and uses of the city's people, even as, perhaps, those desires are expressed through a shrinking of the city's built footprint.[35] That footprint cannot be left to the dictates of fickle and inevitably uneven capitalist invest-ment. Capitalism is a poor guardian or sponsor of urban life. Indeed, it is frequently urban life's biggest enemy (cities made in its image are not cities many of us want to—or even can—be in).

A reorientation of our project—from retrenchment and reinvestment to the Right to the City, that is, putting people's needs and desires and use-values ahead of the needs and desires and exchange values of capital—might just possibly open up a new way not just of living in cities but especially of *making* cities. Such a reorientation would be nothing short of revolutionary. We here in the Rust Belt would not be formerly urban; we would instead begin to realize the promise of the urban.

1   Neil Smith, *Uneven Development: Nature, Capital, and the Production of Space*, 2nd ed. (Oxford: Blackwell, 1990); and David Harvey, *Spaces of Global Capitalism: Towards a Theory of Uneven Geographical Development* (London: Verso, 2006).

2   Karl Marx, *Capital: A Critique of Political Economy*, vol. 1 (New York: International Publishers 1987); Smith, *Uneven Development*; and David Harvey, *The Limits to Capital* (Chicago: University of Chicago Press, 1982).

3   The idea of "creative destruction" originated with Marx and Friedrich Engels, particularly in *The Communist Manifesto*, to signify the way that capital accumulation had to proceed by "battering down all barriers" and remaking the landscape in a manner more suitable for "accumulation's sake" (as Marx later put it), but was popularized and reworked by Schumpeter in *Capitalism, Socialism, and Democracy* and in other works. See *The Communist Manifesto* (London: Verso, 1998); and *Capitalism, Socialism, and Democracy* (New York: Harper Perennial, 1962). In Marx's hands, creative destruction was a means of understanding how the building up of surpluses was always also a process of social and geographical annihilation. For Schumpeter it was something far more admirable: the constant innovation necessarily at the heart of capitalism meant not that barriers to accumulation were merely destroyed, but that they were creatively destroyed. In the process of wiping out old worlds, new and usually better ones were made. While the Schumpeterian version of creative destruction has been picked up and not infrequently celebrated in the business press—often in articles that weirdly echo Stalinist recipes for omelet-making—the development of a critical theory of creative destruction, one true to its origins in an analysis rather than a celebration of capitalism, has been most advanced by David Harvey. He has shown clearly how the constant wiping out of barriers to capitalist accumulation always entails the simultaneous construction of a new landscape—a new spatial arrangement—that itself will be subject to the gale-force winds of capitalist destruction. Marshall Berman has shown just what such winds of destruction feel like for working-class and bourgeois denizens of modernism alike. I am less concerned with affect and feeling and far more concerned with what creative destruction means for the very ability of some people to live, especially since such destruction is both uneven and place-specific, with whole cities and towns—places where people live and feel and are rooted in a thick soil of social relations—often made (nearly) obsolete overnight.

     See also Harvey, *The Limits to Capital*; Harvey, *Spaces of Global Capitalism*; David Harvey, "The Urban Process Under Capitalism: A Framework for Analysis," *International Journal of Urban and Regional Research* 2 (1978): 101–31; David Harvey, *The Urban Experience* (Oxford: Blackwell, 1989); David Harvey, *Spaces of Capital: Towards a Critical Geography* (London: Routledge, 2001); David Harvey, *A Brief History of Neoliberalism* (Oxford: Oxford University Press, 2005); David Harvey, *The Enigma of Capital: And the Crises of Capitalism* (Oxford: Oxford University Press, 2010); and Marshall Berman, *All That Is Solid Melts into Air: The Experience of Modernity* (London: Verso, 1984).

4   Don Mitchell, "A History of Homelessness—A Geography of Control: The Production of Spaces of Order and Marginality in Johnstown, Pennsylvania" (master's thesis, Pennsylvania State University, 1989); Don Mitchell, "Heritage, Landscape, and the Production of Community: Consensus History and Its Alternatives in Johnstown, Pennsylvania,"

Pennsylvania History 59 (1992): 198–226; Don Mitchell, "Public Housing in Single-Industry Towns: Changing Landscapes of Paternalism," in *Place/Culture/Representation*, eds. James Duncan and David Ley (London: Routledge, 1993), 110–27; and Don Mitchell, *Cultural Geography: A Critical Introduction* (Oxford: Blackwell, 2000), 91–99.

5   Barry Bluestone and Bennett Harrison, *The Deindustrialization of America* (New York: Basic Books, 1982); and Bennett Harrison and Barry Bluestone, *The Great U-Turn: Corporate Restructuring and the Polarizing of America* (New York: Basic Books, 1988).

6   Smith, *Uneven Development*, 128.

7   Marx, *Capital*, 168.

8   On resistance to deindustrialization, see Staughton Lynd, *The Fight Against Shutdowns: Youngstown's Steel Mill Closings* (San Pedro, Calif.: Singlejack Books, 1982).

9   Harvey, *The Limits to Capital*.

10   Harvey L. Molotch, "The City as Growth Machine: Towards a Political Economy of Place," *American Journal of Sociology* 82, no. 2 (1976): 309–30; John R. Logan and Harvey L. Molotch, *Urban Fortunes: The Political Economy of Place* (Berkeley: University of California Press, 1988); Susan E. Clarke and Gary L. Gaile, *The Work of Cities* (Minneapolis: University of Minnesota Press, 1998); and Andrew E. G. Jonas and David Wilson, eds., *The Urban Growth Machine: Critical Perspectives Two Decades Later* (Albany: SUNY Press, 1999).

11   Tim Hall and Phil Hubbard, eds., *The Entrepreneurial City: Geographies of Politics, Regime and Representation* (Chicester, U.K.: John Wiley and Sons, 1998); Andrew Jonas and Linda McCarthy, "Urban Management and Regeneration in the United States: State Intervention or Redevelopment at All Costs?" *Local Government Studies* 35 (2009): 299–314; and Andrew Jonas and Linda McCarthy, "Redevelopment at All Costs? A Critical Review and Examination of the American Model of Urban Management and Regeneration," in *Urban Regeneration Management: International Perspectives*, eds. John Diamond, Joyce Liddle, Alan Southern, and Philip Osei (New York: Routledge, 2009), 31–60.

12   Perhaps no better evidence of the faddishness of such efforts can be found than Richard Florida's recent announcement that some cities are lost causes, will never be able to attract the creative class or even be creative, and ought to just give up the ghost. Even the creative class, Florida recently announced, has no hope of saving Detroit. See Richard Florida, "How the Crash Will Reshape America," *Atlantic Monthly*, March 2009, http://www.atlanticmonthly.com/magazine/print/2009/03. The "economic troubadour" reference is from Alec MacGillis, "The Ruse of the Creative Class," *American Prospect*, January 4, 2010, http://prospect.org/cs/articles?article=the_ruse_of_the_creative_class. For a full critique of Florida's urban sales pitch, see Jamie Peck, "Struggling with the Creative Class," *International Journal of Urban and Regional Research* 29 (2005): 740–70.

13   Sharon Zukin, *The Cultures of Cities* (Oxford: Blackwell, 1995).

14   This line might be physical, defined by some old piece of infrastructure like a dripping, rusting highway viaduct, or it might be cartographic, defined by the boundaries of a tax-increment financing district or some other modern form of redlining.

15   Youngstown is at the forefront of the shrinking cities movement in the United States. For details on what it has accomplished, see Hunter Morrison's essay in this volume. The movement has gone global and particularly has adherents in the formerly industrial areas of Germany. See "Shrinking Cities," http://www.shrinkingcities.com/index.php?L=1.

16   All quotations in this and the next two paragraphs are from John Russo and James Rhodes, "A Renaissance for Whom?: Youngstown and Its Neighborhoods," Center for Working-Class Studies at Youngstown State University, http://cwcs.ysu.edu/resources/CWCS-publications/renaissance. John Russo is the founder and longtime codirector of the Center for Working-Class Studies, an innovative center that brings together working people; scholars from across the sciences, social sciences, and humanities; artists; and others in collaborative efforts to both rescue working-class life from the condescension of history and to explore

how working-class prerogatives must be central to any revival of socially just geographies. A longtime Youngstown resident deeply committed to its history and future, Russo is a labor economist by training and a professor in Youngstown's Warren P. Williamson, Jr. College of Business Administration. James Rhodes is a visiting scholar at the Center for Working-Class Studies as well as a Simon Research Fellow in sociology at the University of Manchester.

17   Those of us familiar with other cities—like Hartford or Syracuse, for example—could tell very similar tales of two cities, as universities and other organizations and institutions lead development efforts that have significant if uneven effects around campuses or in designated districts (especially those with remnant infrastructure ripe for gentrification), while other neighborhoods remain as deeply troubled as ever.

18   Harvey, "The Urban Process Under Capitalism," 124.

19   Ibid. See also Edward Soja, *Seeking Spatial Justice* (Minneapolis: University of Minnesota Press, 2010), 88.

20   Neil Brenner, Peter Marcuse, and Margit Mayer, eds., *Cities for People and Not for Profit: Critical Urban Theory and the Right to the City* (New York: Routledge, 2011).

21   David Harvey, "The Right to the City," *New Left Review* 53 (2008): 23–40; and Peter Marcuse, "From Critical Urban Theory to the Right to the City," *City* 13 (2009): 185–97.

22   For a brilliant introduction to Lefebvre's life and work, see Andy Merrifield, *Henri Lefebvre: A Critical Introduction* (London: Routledge, 2006).

23   Mark Purcell's reduction of the right to the city to primarily a right to participation is therefore faulty since it leaves aside (indeed rules out-of-bounds) the question of participating in what, and thus in essence recapitulates a call for little more than participatory planning. His rejection of any class analysis is also deeply problematic in the way it fails to understand the structuring force relations of capitalist accumulation in city development while also turning attention from the differential, class-based effects such accumulation has; the effect is to promote a right to the city presumably for all but really for the middle classes. Other theorists of the right to the city, especially Marcuse, have made it plain that the question of the right to what is as important as the question of who is to possess this right, and that focusing on the fate of and organizing with the working class is vital for any progressive Right to the City movement. See Henri Lefebvre, "The Right to the City," in *Writings on Cities*, trans. and eds. Eleonore Kofman and Elizabeth Lebas (Oxford: Blackwell, 1996), 59–181; Mark Purcell, "Excavating Lefebvre: The Right to the City and its Urban Politics of the Inhabitant," *GeoJournal* 55 (2002): 99–108; Mark Purcell, "Citizenship and the Right to the Global City: Reimagining the Capitalist World Order," *International Journal of Urban and Regional Research* 27 (2003): 564–90; and Marcuse, "From Critical Urban Theory to the Right to the City,"

24   Lefebvre, "The Right to the City," 173–74.

25   Ibid., 158.

26   Which is not to say that some form of accumulation is not necessary. Indeed, as Harvey has long argued, urbanism is predicated on the creation of a surplus. The right to the city, he thus argues, entails democratic control over the production, distribution, and use of that surplus.

27   Lefebvre, "The Right to the City," 179.

28   Harvey, *A Brief History of Neoliberalism*.

29   Kafui Attoh, "What Kind of a Right Is the Right to the City?" *Progress in Human Geography* 35 (2001), 669–85.

30   Ibid. Jeremy Waldron, *Liberal Rights: Collected Papers, 1981–1991* (Cambridge: Cambridge University Press, 1993).

31   Don Mitchell and Nik Heynen, "The Geography of Survival and the Right to the City: Speculations on Surveillance, Legal Innovation, and the Criminalization of Intervention," *Urban Geography* 30 (2009): 611–32.

32   Attoh, "What Kind of a Right Is the Right to the City?"; and Marcuse, "From Critical Urban Theory to the Right to the City."

33   For more on the struggle for the right to centrality and participatory planning, see Purcell, "Excavating Lefebvre." See also Purcell, "Citizenship and the Right to the Global City"; and Harvey, "The Right to the City," 23.

34   UN-HABITAT, http://www.unhabitat.org/categories.asp?catid=584; Right to the City Alliance, http://www.righttothecity.org; and Brenner et al., *Cities for People and Not for Profit*.

35   Lefebvre, "Right to the City," 103.

Strange Attractors: The Catalytic Agency of Form

Roger Sherman

"[T]he action of Russia…is a riddle wrapped in a mystery inside
an enigma; but…there is a key. That key is…[self] interest."
—Winston Churchill

Previous page: Fig. 1.
TargetPlay: aerial view

The "formerly urban," as it has been coined, becomes productive
only when considered a symptom rather than a condition. Its import
is greatest when not exclusively in reference to a context of loss—of
jobs, population, and community life, such as characterizes Rust Belt
cities—but to a largely unrecognized shift in the fact that the effects and
benefits of the urban are being produced by alternative means.[1] This
is as true of growing and thriving metropolitan areas like Los Angeles
as of so-called shrinking cities like Buffalo, which have weak markets
localized within them (i.e., South L.A.), consistent with David Harvey's
contention that it is in the nature of the late capitalist city to develop
unevenly.[2] Of greater significance is its tacit acknowledgment that an
economic and cultural phase change has taken place that has funda-
mentally affected urban life as we know it. A radical redistribution of
resources has caused a general restructuring of processes of urbanization, altering the logistical regimens and commuting patterns—and by
extension the daily schedules, habits, and lifestyles—of most who live
and/or work in urbanized areas. Those who shape the city, however,
have been slow to react, with changes in urban form occurring more as
a function of purely market-driven development rather than in ways
shaped by architects who recognize the import and potentials of those
changes. As a result, the formerly urban environs that one physically
inhabits seems increasingly disaggregated, like The Matrix, even as
plans representing its future seem impossibly uniform, polite, and
ordered, constrained by outdated assumptions about urban life that are
embedded in zoning policies. And neither exhibits any resemblance
to the new, linked but self-organized forms of collectivity, which the
Internet so flexibly and dynamically facilitates.

Seen in this context, the formerly urban reflects the fact that both
investment and participation in the physical space of the city itself are
no longer presumptive but rather are increasingly discretionary. The
ease and speed of online social and economic arrangements have had
the effect of transforming the notion of community to one that is ever
more specific and differentiated, and at the same time conditional and
itinerant, to a degree that the city itself—at least in its present form—
is not. Whatever alternative means of producing the urban are developed must therefore begin by identifying the kinds of community
and logistical arrangements in the making that have incubated under

this new medium, with the aim of catalyzing and then reifying those versions in real space. To do so requires moving beyond conventional tools of urban definition (such as solid and void, land-use classification, etc.), and employing other visual/experiential mediums that traditionally have been only subservient to those of architecture and landscape. In Los Angeles, for instance, only 25 percent of land is actually occupied by buildings, while at the same time that city possesses the lowest amount of public open space per capita of any major North American city.[3] The apparent lack of concurrence between these two factoids suggests, among other things, that contemporary urban form is more complexly defined than can be delineated in simple, binary distinctions (e.g., building vs. landscape, public vs. private). It also points to the fact that the general lack of compactness of the twentieth-century metropolis is not necessarily commensurate with a lower mean population; in fact, many cities, like Los Angeles, have experienced only growth. On one level, the formerly urban is therefore a reflection of the preference for a more privatized, aleatory, disaggregated way of life: to live in one place, work in another, shop in yet a third, and so on. Enabled by the automobile and embodied in the variegated patterns and textures of suburbia, density is no longer driven by need, either for convenience or proximity, but by desire.

The absence of density in the suburban (and now so-called postsuburban) model is, however, belied by an ever-growing virtual density of knowledge about population habits, demographics, stakeholders, ecologies, and property values (to name just a few) of those very areas. While for most of the recorded history of cities the natural and direct correspondence between density and intensity has been assumed, the radical prophesy revealed by geographic information systems (GIS) and other sensing technologies is that today, at least, the relationship between concentrations of form and those of activities and resources is indirect at best. GIS has brought with it the realization that not only is density not the automatic outcome of intensity, but intensity—often visible only as an overlay of data sets—can and does result in projects that develop (or "pop up") as naturally occurring phenomena, where one might least expect them, away from areas of existing density. More specifically, it enables one to predict and therefore deliberately strategize the future (in terms of desirability, growth, etc.) of specific locales, by identifying and then correlating characteristics, such as ecological and movement patterns and behaviors, to potential markets/audiences. Through such a correlative process, larger collective patterns or tendencies may be detected that are either hidden in plain sight or in the making. The value of this information, to entrepreneurs and architects alike, lies not in its indexing or expression in real space (i.e., the so-called datascapes that have become de rigueur in certain architectural circles), but rather in the analysis and identification of exquisite coincidences of activities and characteristics occurring in specific zones or points of overlap or intensity. While the source of these hot spots used to be obvious upon simple visual inspection (i.e., proximity or access to views or natural resources), GIS and other sensing technologies have made it possible to "find" places that are seemingly without self-evident value but whose geo-data reveals them to possess latent but complementary traits and phenomena, whose collocation implies potential (i.e., developable) worth.

This worth is not self-fulfilling, however; it is contingent upon successfully leveraging those facts and circumstances through design strategy, bringing them into play in the form of a robust combination of itineraries. The strictly forensic "connecting of dots" between factoids is insufficient to precipitate future action. The design of the project that results from this scripting becomes a kind of conceit, or pretext, by which to invite, induce, and ultimately orchestrate those very same motives, means, and opportunities—be they untapped catchment areas, foot traffic patterns, or access to water supply. At the same time, it must do so in a way that only prefigures, but does not prescribe, those prospective itineraries. This process of extrapolation begins by looking for meaningful coincidences between a given location's "found" characteristics (e.g., resources and proximities) and other more general knowledge of trends, tendencies, or problems that are at large or "in the air," as a means of speculating upon or imagining the identities of the audiences that such synergies might assemble. In this sense, the hot spot follows neither the traditional model of urbanization to succeed, which relies upon connectivity, nor does it assume the self-fulfilling build-it-and-they-will-come growth model of postwar suburbia. Instead, in an era of equivocal urbanity (urbanity without density), it *achieves* or produces its own audience in the way that it parses, manages, and ultimately exploits information toward a peculiar—not conventionally urban—mix of collective life.

To this point in time, those who have been quickest to understand and exploit the value of such geo-data have tended to employ it only to the extent of identifying hot spots simply as locations for specific tenant mixes and precooked business-cum-design strategies—best represented in those developments known as "lifestyle centers." Incubated in Las Vegas's nursery of "varietal urbanisms," these predigested, abridged versions of the urban offer the spectacle of the city (as opposed to actual membership and participation) as the source of their drawing power. Sporting names such as Citywalk and L.A. Live! (with an exclamation mark as if to distinguish it from Los Angeles, or perhaps offering itself as a new and improved version of the original), this model is characterized by a faux density aided and abetted, like any studio back lot, by "random happenings" staged on the hour. Density is reduced to a trope for the city-as-hot-spot, with hyper-variegation acting as a signifier of its diversity. Instruments of consumption more than forums for real exchange, lifestyle centers offer the experience of city life sanitized of risk, unruliness, and social interchange. To dwell on the obviously suspect efficacy of such ventures as bona fide models of collective life, however, is to also ignore the fact of their undeniable attractive power to the public at large—one sourced in the satisfaction of a certain "alt" interest of the suburbanite in urbanism on demand. This has proven to succeed even in areas of declining population and industry, often in the absence of any connectivity to surrounding development.

As a business model, however, the self-contained lifestyle center operates as the social and economic equivalent of a black hole. It is designed only to lure to itself—to succeed *in spite of* rather than to catalyze that which surrounds it. This is largely due to the fact that it offers the *spectacle of the urban*—as opposed to *urbanity itself*—as the source of its drawing power. In contrast to this reduction of the urban to passive gesture and expression, an alternative strategy is emerging: one directed more toward *effect* than (the lifestyle center's) *affect*. As opposed to the lifestyle center's *urbanism-as-spectacle*, the alternative paradigm, which operates as a form of *strange attractor*, is invested in the notion of *spectacle-as-urbanism* (fig. 1). It is the *intensity of experience*—or experience of intensity, rather than of density—that is the source of its power. Like the stone in the children's parable "Stone Soup," the strange attractor purports to be and look like something else (*not* urban), but its intent and underlying effect are, in fact, to precipitate just that: the differing forms of activity that characterize urban life. It accomplishes this, more specifically, by recognizing the Trojan horse–like allure of the marriage of *conceit* and *deceit*.

The strange attractor's conceit-deceit dynamic adeptly exploits the public's insatiable appetite to decipher (its curiosity about curiosity) and to elicit and synthesize the motives, opportunities, and means

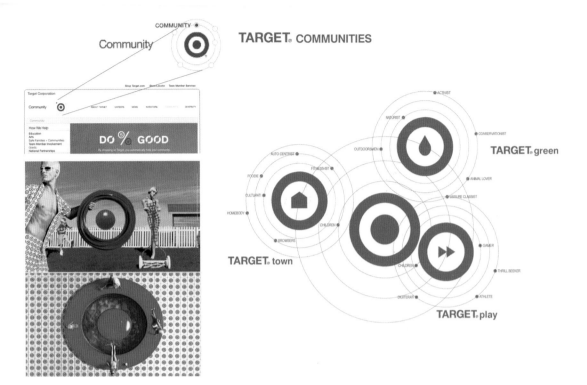

Fig. 2. Target Nation: Thinking Out of the Big Box; Roger Sherman Architecture and Urban Design, with Greg Kochanowski. Project team: Quyen Luong (project manager), John Chavez, Dustin Gramstead, Brendan Muha, Daniel Phillips, Daniel Poei, Ben Ragle, Stephanie Ragle, Amelia Wong, Andrew Benson

necessary to catalyze future action, even amidst contexts and audiences that are ambivalently, if not formerly, urban. Taking a page from the conceptual art movement, the conceit component of this formula is built upon the cunning parsing, interpretation, and correlation of select facts amidst a forest of geo-data ranging from immediate to global (fig. 2). Like a Rorschach test, it transfixes the gaze through a certain semiotic undecidability: a form of not just conceptual but also perceptual puzzle that poses a usually unanswerable query that inspires wonder and intrigue, itching to be "verified in field" or "played" to be figured out.[4] Aimed at no single predetermined identity group, but rather, like the hot spot itself, at finding an unlikely point of tangency shared obliquely by many possible interests, the strange attractor's conceit strengthens its agency even as it weakens its straight-line relation to a single set of logistical demands. As such, it somewhat ironically translates the modernist interest in performance from one defined in terms of optimization and expression to that of the ability to effect, instigate, and even preempt actions beyond itself—appearing as one thing but implying another.

The conceit serves as a form of script out of which an uncommon yet familiar image-ability might emerge, evinced through a peculiar combination of semiotics and visual effects (figs. 3, 4). These are orchestrated through effects and illusions of the sort more commonly employed by the commercial film and advertising industries, in a way that is both popularly accessible and at the same time capable of provoking a strong and lasting emotional response. These forms of visual deception are aimed at manipulating and undermining popularly held assumptions about physics and the physics of perception, such as gravity, perspective, scale, and material association (fig. 5). They lure interest by altering the real through uncanny I-can't-believe-my-eyes visual feats, using techniques such as exaggeration (e.g., distortion, contortion, and overuse), montage (e.g., rematerialization and recombination), stereoscopy (e.g., anamorphism and lenticularity), 2.5D (e.g., alternating between flatness and spatial depth), instability/precariousness, and ambience/ephemera. The visual trickery of stereoscopy, for instance, can be instrumental in enabling the strange attractor to address diverse interests by simultaneously broadcasting one message to the ground-level perspective of not-in-my-backyard-ists; a second to that of the elevated perspective of drivers (prospective

Fig 3. TargetPlay: bird's-eye view

Fig 4. TargetPlay: ground-level view

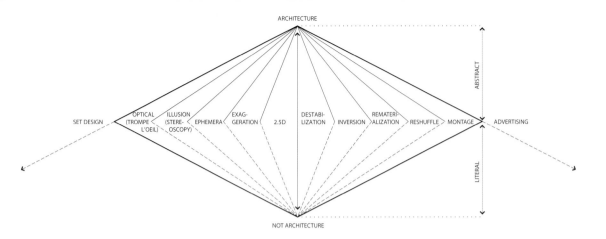

Fig 5. The Attracted Field
(with apologies to Rosalind Krauss)

shoppers) on adjacent freeways; and yet a third to the global audience of Google Earth.

By contrast with mere Vegas-style hucksterism, such sleight of hand is designed not merely to attract attention, but to retain it. Visual effects are used not, as with special effects, to stage experiences that stand apart from the everyday, but rather as one component of a larger semiotic-optical construct aimed at producing an urbanism through its alteration/augmentation of the real (or Frederic Jameson's *hyperreal*). They do not operate as stand-alone, one-line sight gags, but rather work to elicit a *second* (double) *take*—a how-did-they fascination that invites closer and repeated inspection in order to uncover their underlying logic. To sustain this intrigue, these underlying mechanics are deliberately obscure, also reinforcing the enigma of the conceit's own derivation. The combination lends the strange attractor a gnomon-like mix of mesmerization and indifference.[5] Certain of its formal or material properties are literal, deadpan, banal reproductions of the real and familiar, upon which the above-mentioned sleight of hand is then deployed, construing an initial impression of something that is both common and at the same time not quite right—transfixing the gaze and forcing a certain self query ("What's wrong with this picture?") in the spectator. This "tell" operates as something of both an opening gambit and a clue as to its origins. Again, like the Trojan horse, the strange attractor presents itself as something of a puzzle: in the process of being "solved" by the spectator through his/her use and interaction, the puzzle divulges an unexpected political intelligence—an embedded strategy of co-option, not only of the audiences that are critical to

forging its collective (though not conventionally urban) status, but also of the stakeholders necessary to enabling its realization.

The strange attractor employs the direct, literal forms of visual communication with which the public today is conversant, in contrast to the more abstract, geometrical, and planner-ly mediums of architecture and urban design, which are driven, at least of late, more by medium than by message. Here I am not referring to the obdurate, inarguable, assertive dimension of the literal, but rather its preposterous counterpart—what may be termed the "slightly literal"—that has the power to make some laugh and others cry.[6] Because the techniques of the literal are viewed with disdain by much of architectural culture, it is the fields that are conversant with them (e.g., art, advertising, and visual effects) that must be instead increasingly looked to as possessing the sensibility to attract new audiences in ways that the architectural projects with which they are often associated do not. Architecture is focused instead on the expression of interior function and its reconciliation with exterior demands. Indeed, the Los Angeles County Museum of Art (LACMA) did precisely this when it commissioned artists Jeff Koons

Fig 6. Photo of Chris Burden's *Urban Light* (2008), at the Los Angeles County Museum of Art

Fig 7. Photo of Jeff Koons's *Train*, proposed for the Los Angeles County Museum of Art

Top: Fig 8. "Before" view of
Playa Rosa showing existing
shopping center

Bottom: Fig 9. Aerial view from the
southwest of Playa Rosa: cityLAB /
Roger Sherman Architecture and
Urban Design (J. R. Chavez, Elan
Lipson, Joem Sanez, Mike Amaya,
Yilip Kang)

Opposite, top: Fig 10. Diagram of
Playa Rosa stakeholders

Opposite, bottom: Fig 11.
Diagram of Playa Rosa leveraged
infrastructure

and Chris Burden to establish LACMA's public presence and profile
in a way that neither Renzo Piano's well-crafted but mute additions nor
Peter Zumthor's future ones have or will (figs. 6, 7). Likewise, it is not
Gehry's name recognition nor his signature bandshell that has proven
to be the prime attraction of Chicago's Millennium Park, but Anish
Kapoor's *Cloud Gate* and its mesmerizing visual effects—this in the
absence of any programmatic pretext.

The "slightly literal" offers architects—and just as equally urban
designers—a powerful delivery mechanism by which to smuggle in disciplinary relevance. As opposed to supplanting the real altogether with an
abstract, entirely virtually conceived alternative (architecture's current
tendency) or, at the other end of the spectrum, settling for its mere repli-
cation (the everyday), the strange attractor's allure and its agency lie in
altering reality—adding to or taking things away from it—as if to serve
as an object lesson in the transformative "before vs. after" potential of

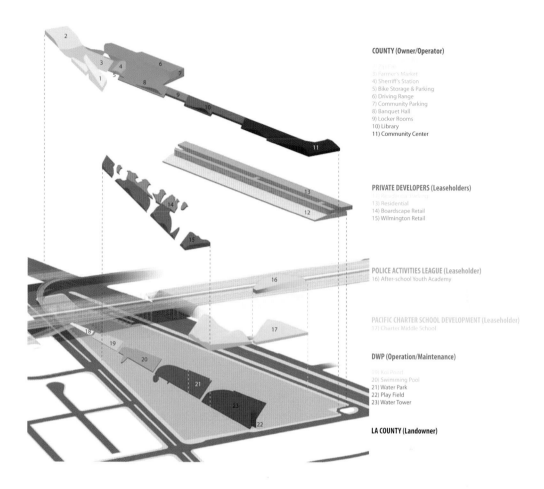

COUNTY (Owner/Operator)

3) Farmer's Market
4) Sheriff's Station
5) Bike Storage & Parking
6) Driving Range
7) Community Parking
8) Banquet Hall
9) Locker Rooms
10) Library
11) Community Center

PRIVATE DEVELOPERS (Leaseholders)

13) Residential
14) Boardscape Retail
15) Wilmington Retail

POLICE ACTIVITIES LEAGUE (Leaseholder)
16) After-school Youth Academy

PACIFIC CHARTER SCHOOL DEVELOPMENT (Leaseholder)
17) Charter Middle School

DWP (Operation/Maintenance)

19) Koi Pond
20) Swimming Pool
21) Water Park
22) Play Field
23) Water Tower

LA COUNTY (Landowner)

LEVERAGED INFRASTRUCTURE

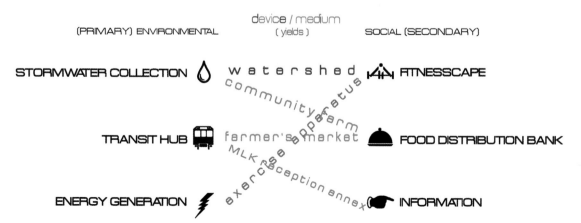

(PRIMARY) ENVIRONMENTAL   device / medium (yields)   SOCIAL (SECONDARY)

STORMWATER COLLECTION   watershed   FITNESSCAPE

TRANSIT HUB   farmer's market   FOOD DISTRIBUTION BANK

ENERGY GENERATION   INFORMATION

community farm   exercise apparatus   MLK reception annex

cities. Like the makeover, its effects are achieved simply and cheaply, with available matter. This includes weakening or transgressing architecture's conventional disciplinary bounds by subjecting it to material logics and practices that are more commonly associated with the atmospheres of the urban (versus architecture's address of the urban typically through solid-void relationships), as R. E. Somol has pointed out, such as lighting, infrastructural elements, graphics, and planting.[7]

The strange attractor is embodied in Playa Rosa, a proposal for a consolidated public service hub located in the Watts neighborhood of South L.A. Initiated by Los Angeles County, Playa Rosa is aimed at revitalizing an area of the city that has suffered a succession of ills—from near-catastrophic flooding due to its low-lying elevation in the Compton Creek watershed, to social unrest in 1967 and 1992 that resulted from the disaggregating effects of four decades of flight to more affluent outer-ring suburbs. Most recently these problems have come to include a high rate of childhood obesity and diabetes, traceable to a lack of public activity—a symptom of a high incidence of gang violence. All of the above are emblematized in the existing site, whose 15 acres are occupied by a failing commercial center that includes six fast-food outlets (fig. 8). At the seeming epicenter of this perfect storm of environmental, social, and public health problems, Playa Rosa puts forth a deceptively simple conceit—that of an urban beach (fig. 9). Both unprecedented and of a political significance immediately graspable by the community, this beach—like the real one 10 miles

Opposite, top: Fig. 12. View of Playa Rosa looking north from the Police Activities League

Opposite, bottom: Fig. 13. View of Playa Rosa looking south from Rosa Parks Station

Above: Fig 14. Diagram of social justice

to the west, which is seldom visited by local residents (who own on average less than one car per household)—cuts across existing social and spatial statics, undermining previous models of identity politics and special interest.

The intelligence of such a strategy, well recognized by the project's sponsor, is that the beach and the public components associated with it (water reclamation, childcare center, library, pool/water park, etc.)— paid for through a combination of federal and state moneys—are but the tip of a larger underlying scenario-cum-business plan to attract private investment (fig. 10).[8] Privately backed land uses—greengrocer, work-force housing, charter school, police activities league—comple- ment their public counterparts in enabling the itineraries that are essential to supporting Playa Rosa's health and wellness scenario. These include providing a safe but active place for commuting neigh- borhood residents to leave and pick up their children on their way to and from the adjacent transit station, and attracting medical workers to the area by establishing a location that both creates and secures its own desirability as a place to live and recreate, despite the current instability of its surrounds. Unlike its strategic antecedents (New York's Central Park or Paris's Place Vendôme), however, Playa Rosa's salient image- ability is tied not to amenity as much as to *ambience*: an intensity of overall effect that is the result of employing not one but a full gamut of mediums. Its power comes from using these interchangeably and even transgressively with respect to the "architecture" itself, whereby the material logic of one discipline is assumed by another (i.e., landscape is treated primarily as a graphics problem; building as a landscape problem, and so on). In short, Playa Rosa *affects* collective life through its varied types of *effects*. At the same time, the visceral intensity of the enclave model from which it borrows is opened up to and inclusive of a wider and less predefined group of audiences.

Though located at what geo-data suggests is a naturally occurring hot spot (the site is near Rosa Parks Station, a major regional light- rail node), Playa Rosa achieves critical mass as an urban catalyst not by falsely relying on the assumed public status of infrastructure for its drawing power but by instead looking to expand the conven- tional, single-purpose role of "hard" infrastructural networks (in this case, transportation, energy supply, and storm-water collection) and leveraging them in the service of a parallel set of "soft" or social ones (fig. 11).[9] Though clearly a conceit, at another level the urban beach facilitates an organizational and morphological synergy between the two networks. It accomplishes this, however, without investing its visual appearance in the overt expression of (i.e., the diagram of) those systems at work.[10] Instead, those linkages are sublimated in service of a singular image-ability, whose literality is directed toward a more rhetorical end, "operating" as a working symbol of the health and wellness needs of an at-risk community—healthy food sources, fitness landscapes, community programs, and safe havens for at-risk youth— and, at a deeper level, of social and environmental justice (figs. 12–14).

1   Roger Sherman, "Urbanity Without Density" (lecture, "Formerly Urban: Projecting Rust Belt Futures" conference, Syracuse University School of Architecture, Syracuse, N.Y., October 13–14, 2010).

2   David Harvey, *Spaces of Global Capitalism: A Theory of Uneven Geographical Development* (London: Verso, 2006).

3   In Los Angeles, there are 1.1 acres per 1,000 residents. In ten other major American cities, there are on average 10 acres per 1,000 residents. A mere 5 percent of L.A.'s land is devoted to parks, compared to Boston's 7 percent and New York's 14 percent. See Los Angeles Neighborhood Land Trust, http://www.lanlt.org.

4   The Leaning Tower of Pisa is one, if accidental, example of this. Its notoriety comes not from the skill of its techniques of design or execution but rather from the mesmerizing spectacle of its instability based on circumstance.

5   Roger Sherman, "Yes is More," in *L.A. Under the Influence: The Hidden Logic of Urban Property* (Minneapolis: University of Minnesota Press, 2010), xv.

6   Mark Linder, *Nothing Less than Literal: Architecture after Minimalism* (Cambridge, Mass.: MIT Press, 2004).

7   Stan Allen, "Urbanism without Architecture," in *Points + Lines: Diagrams and Projects for the City* (New York: Princeton Architectural Press, 1999), 140.

8   Federal and state financiers include Los Angeles County, Los Angeles Department of Water and Power, Metropolitan Water District of Southern California, and Los Angeles County Metropolitan Transportation Authority.

9   This is supported by a parallel county-initiated strategy to consolidate its widely dispersed properties into a limited number of "constituent service centers" intended to establish long-overdue places of public gathering and investment in fragmented urban neighborhoods in need of revitalization.

10   As distinguished from landscape urbanism, which promotes design as an outcome and expression of (ecological) processes.

Pits and Piles in the Non-Concept City: Luzerne County, Pennsylvania

Edward Mitchell

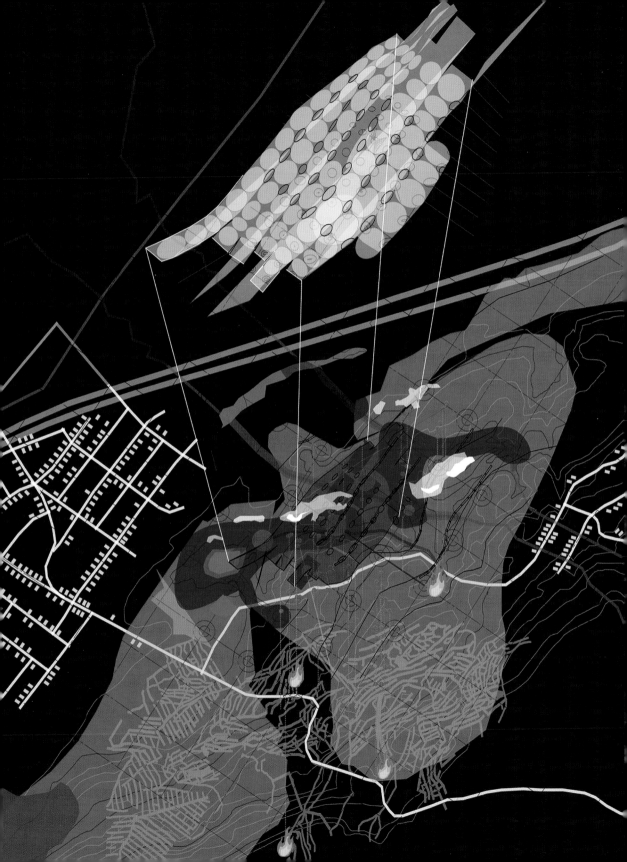

"Under construction everything is half complete. In ruins
all is complete."
—*Werckmeister Harmonies* (2000)

The Shadow's Nowhere

Cutting across on the Interstate 80 eastern approach, the Wyoming
Valley in Luzerne County, Pennsylvania, appears, like a painting by Lucio
Fontana, as a crescent wound in the Appalachians (fig. 1). The valley is
a particular American form of nowhere. Its largest city, Scranton, is the
location for NBC's *The Office*, a comic take on the quotidian dramas
of ordinary people employed in a dying paper industry. But to talk about
the area as a network of cities and towns is inaccurate. When Rem
Koolhaas spoke of "conceptual Nevadas," where all laws of architecture
are suspended, he may not have envisioned the "conceptual Scrantons,"
of Becket-like waiting rooms, pointless conference rooms, static loading
docks, and shale pilings and smoking hills of the valley. [1] The elimination
of form leads nowhere.

Mining was once Luzerne County's chief economic engine and the
cause of historic urbanization. It remains culturally significant to the
area but has become a major liability to development. Coal-mining
properties were excluded from Superfund designation, and so vast
acres of the valley remain compromised without recourse to federal
funding. Over the years several people have been killed or injured
falling into open pits, while the extreme landscapes of copper lakes,
smoking hillsides, and stripped slopes provoke an ambivalent aesthetic
response. For nearly twenty years, the Earth Conservancy (EC)—
a nonprofit organization with a board of local citizens—has successfully
reclaimed large tracts of the 16,000 acres under its stewardship. Parcels
owned by the EC are typically approached off winding, unpaved roads,
where one discovers enormous piles of slag that resemble the pyramids
of a lost civilization. The by-products of the mining process are sublime
testimonials to a dead industry.

Natural gas companies have begun land speculation in Pennsylvania-
New York border towns in the Marcellus Shale, 20 miles north of
Luzerne County. New wealth associated with both rising land values
and the energy industry may drift south. This enterprise may be
curtailed by protests against fracking—the hydraulic fracturing of
rock to obtain fossil fuels—which threatens an already strained local
populace's aquifer and, by extrapolation, the entire drinking supply
of eastern Pennsylvania. While northeast Pennsylvania appears to be

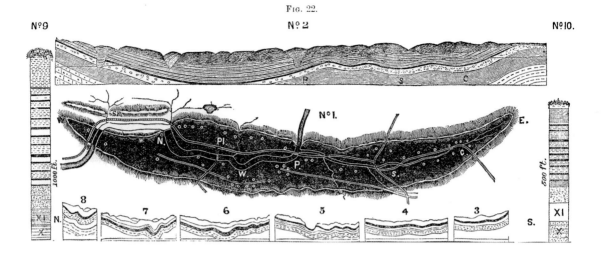

Fig. 1. The Northern or Wyoming Coal Field, from Samuel Harries Daddow and Benjamin Bannan, *Coal, Iron, and Oil; or, The Practical American Miner* (1866)

nowhere, it is also the central trucking distribution center for eastern retail markets. Nearby Hazelton has rehabilitated similar properties for distribution including Michaels (the arts and crafts stores), OfficeMax, and Walgreens.

As principal of Edward Mitchell Architects, my original task was to develop a plan for 500 acres of EC property with the environmental consulting group Vita Nuova. Instead of a plan we recognized that the volatile nature of the site and its scale required a more flexible strategy than making conventional projections on a limited parcel. This observation meant that a broader framework for the project would expand to include close to 10,000 acres for future development. Details like the Mine Fire Project were developed after this study as part of the group Komanda, codirected by Doug Gauthier and in collaboration with a group of engineers and environmentalists.

Degradation caused by mining exaggerates the valley scar. Altering such negative images has been a long-standing concern. The Glen Alden Coal Company, once the largest of these operations, distinguished its coal by spraying it blue and sponsored the famous 1930s radio show *The Shadow*. The Shadow, a Princeton grad who dressed like an architect in black suit, black cape, and red scarf, originally was the protector of Wall Street, battling unethical businessmen. The EC's headquarters sits adjacent to the Huber Breaker, an old coal-processing plant that serves as the most visible architecture of what is essentially an extractive industrial process. Only the Newport-area mines contain enough concentrated, readily available coal to make future extraction viable. Today new economic flows will have to be established. The valley needs new forms of energy and a new energy image.

The Vita Nuova framework plan for the valley was originally presented to the public at Luzerne County Community College two weeks after the 2008 market crash. Over sixty-five developers and city, state, and federal government officials—including Paul Kanjorski, U.S. Representative and member of the Subcommittee on Financial Institutions and Consumer Credit—attended. Kanjorski, who would later be defeated in 2010, warned in the public meeting that the market collapse was far greater than anyone had foreseen. What the future held, apparently, only the Shadow knew.

Boring Thoughts

Geology is fate. The Wyoming Valley formed during the Pennsylvania Era 323–290 million years BCE, when glacial ice and meltwater scoured the underlying bedrock. Nelson Horatio Darton speculated that a large stagnant ice mass occupied the valley after the glacial terminus receded north, though other geologists contend that there is no evidence that such a lake ever existed. The valley is hemmed in by drumlins of the Wisconsin Till, which is characterized by rock formations of "poor to multimodal sorting, unstratified to crudely stratified"—an apt description of the present physical and political conditions of the area.[2]

"History is but agreed fiction, but there is much realism in the fiction, while here all evidences of peoples, of civilizations, powerful society organizations that rose, flourished and passed away, concerning whom we have no tradition," reports local historian Henry C. Bradsby. "All life is but swift change."[3] The Nanticoke Tribe settled here when their Maryland hunting territories were spoiled by colonial settlement. The Appalachians' striated ridges, the tortuous courses of their transverse passes, a heavy forest, and dense undergrowth were barriers to America's westward expansion. "The ability to think," Bradsby observes, "comes largely of soil and climate."[4]

The eighteenth-century discovery of anthracite, which is harder to burn than the more common bitumen coal, is told in Luzerne County legend. Necho Allen, a local farmer, set a fire in his hearth, which was dug into the surrounding earth. "Several hours later I was awakened by summer-like heat," he reports. "Then I saw that the solid earth all about me seemed to be afire." The event ignited "a strange effulgence,"[5] an eternal flame—or one that lasted, at least, until the 1959 Knox Mine flood, marking the essential end of the already diminished industry.

The thickness of the Wyoming Valley's coal beds varies. The deepest coal strata reach 1,700 feet near the Dundee Shaft, close to Nanticoke. Boring samples are cuts in time. Clocking backward at the No. 4 Shaft of the Kingston Coal Company reads: Orchard vein, 4.5 feet; Lance vein, 6.5 feet; Hillman vein, 10 feet; Five-foot vein, 5 feet; Four-foot vein, 4 feet; Six-foot vein, 6 feet; Eleven-foot vein, 11 feet; Cooper vein, 7.5 feet; Bennett vein, 12 feet; Ross vein, 10 feet; Red Ash vein, 9 feet.[6] Folds in the valley structure are pleats in time, where intensified pressure on the deposits hardened the material, formed the characteristic valley patterns, and informed the resultant techniques for extracting anthracite.

In current land-reclamation practice in the central region of the valley, sand and gravel are sorted and separated from shale tailings. Earthmovers spread the shale to make roads, while large acres of repurposed land are covered with four feet of topsoil and seeded in anticipation of new development. The newly greened-up sites might later be paved over for parking lots to service potential commercial development. The process seems to be a futile exercise to reverse entropy in order to restore pulverized gray piles of culm into distinct strata. It is not entirely clear if artificial restratification is, in fact, sustainable. While burying or recycling waste may be one means of reconnecting these sites into an existing urban network, one can also imagine more sublime practices of land reformation: vast fields of black shale raked in rows and furrows that would appear like some colossal Japanese Zen garden or a land art project as conceived by Frank Stella.

The Urban(e)

While the physical form of the region's cities and towns may have declined, the Luzerne Valley remains a significant *urban* site and a test case for the twenty-first century's mobile economies. The conventional tools of the architect can be overwhelmed in these situations. The city is in constant flux, subject to economic vicissitudes. Architecture remains its *other*. This difference commonly pits the urban forces of modernism—economic volatility, scientific invention and innovation, infrastructural change, etc.—against architecture's formally urban project and its semantic and structuralist discourse.

Little of the valley qualifies as a city, making the landscape difficult to describe. The area's physical qualities fall outside of architecture's

Fig. 2. "The Tragic Scene," from
Sebastiano Serlio, *The Five Books of
Architecture*

Fig 3. "The Comic Scene," from
Sebastiano Serlio, *The Five Books of
Architecture*

Fig. 4. "The Satyric Scene," from
Sebastiano Serlio, *The Five Books of
Architecture*

linguistic paradigms. This conceptual linkage between language and the city is exemplified in Sebastiano Serlio's *Five Books of Architecture* (figs. 2–4). "This system" of city structure, primarily military and defensive, Grahame Shane writes, "of walls and taboos is built into the structure of the English language."[7] Serlio divides the urban network into discrete theatrical settings for, in descending order, the Noble or Tragic City, the Comic City, and the Satyric or Pastoral City with their corresponding discourses. Serlio's urban system is *urbane*. Inhabitants of his various cities should demonstrate "good manners," an ability to follow appropriate discourse and put things in their proper place, no matter whether they are city sophisticates or country squires. To do otherwise, to mix up behaviors and syntax, would be to demonstrate improper behavior like some "rustic" country cousin.

Does a Satyric citizen show good form? The three cities are bound together by a road running down the center of each perspective, signaling the emergence of a connective network that will ultimately undermine distinct identities. In the Noble and Comic Cities, the paved road's grid positions buildings, giving them order and meaning. But on closer inspection the Satyric City's gridded road reads either as chunks of sod cut and removed in anticipation of construction or as the broken fragments of an antiquated paving system. The Satyric City sits ambiguously on the brink of urban development or its aftermath, a fitting stage for its inhabitants suspended between culture and the more base animal passions of the world of the satyr.

Ebenezer Howard's diagram for "A Group of Slumless, Smokeless Cities" from *To-morrow: A Peaceful Path to Real Reform*, in contrast, describes a polycentric urban network of cities, towns, and farms connected by rail, canals, and roads, as well as institutions that fall outside the expected concerns of the rational planner—homes for waifs and inebriates, epileptic farms, and insane asylums (fig. 5). Serlio's drawings are exemplary of urban design (small fragments or stage sets for various urban activities), while Howard's drawing describes city theory (the definition of the normative, or what a city should be).[8] Where Serlio's notion of city was proprietary, urbanism is not: urbanism is not a place, but a system that binds the metropolis, the city, the town, the village, and the hamlet. Like Howard's linked connector or Serlio's road, urbanism should not be equated with the city proper as it has the capacity to break strict structural interpretations of discrete architectural types, while it is potentially destructive of city form and a motivated relationship of linguistic signs.[9]

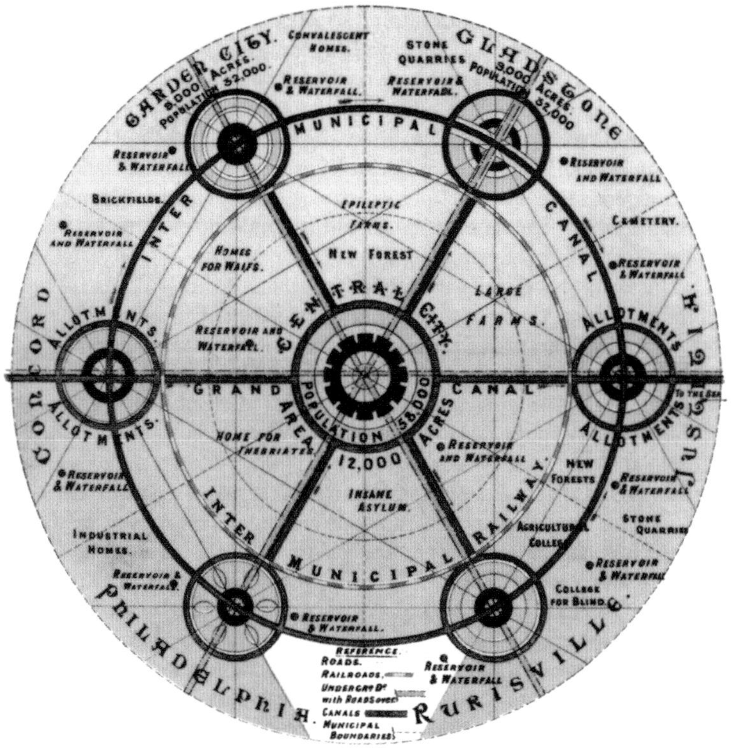

Patches and Dead Zones

The small settlements in the valley resemble the nodes in Howard's polycentric system. During the height of Pennsylvania mining, these small "patch towns" of as few as five hundred people developed adjacent to the pits and breakers so that employees could walk to work. But while the Garden City was made up of self-sustaining community units, the mining companies often owned the patches; the void of the pits, rather than a coherent infrastructure, bound the communities together. The "patches" isolated from their productive relationship to the pits now send mixed signals. The compact urban pattern of the communities of Warrior Run, Sugar Notch, and Korn Krest, Pennsylvania, corresponding to current conventions of sustainable pedestrian-based density, is an asset; but it is also a limitation, producing redundant town services and restrictions on planning initiatives and development. The patches maintain their unique identities in part because they were historically segregated to prevent the miners from forming unions. The valley's native tongue was a local patois of more than twenty-six different languages, Welsh, German, Irish, Russian, Ukrainian, Lithuanian, Polish, Ruthenian, Hungarian,

Fig. 5. "A Group of Slumless, Smokeless Cities," from Ebenezer Howard, *To-morrow: A Peaceful Path to Real Reform* (1898)

Fig. 6. Concrete City, 1914

Lebanese, Syrian, Greek, Slovenian, Croatian, Serbian, and Tyrolean among them. There are over 150 ethnic churches in the area.

One of the region's "model" company towns, Concrete City, constructed by the Delaware, Lackawanna and Western Coal Company in 1911, consisted of twenty-two two-story buildings facing a central green with a wading pool, tennis courts, playground, baseball field, and small pavilion (fig. 6). It is believed to be the first tract-housing project in the United States, anticipating a century of experimentation in prefabrication. The lack of an adequate septic system and concrete's tendency to absorb moisture forced the abandonment of the city in 1924. The city was set up for demolition, but one hundred sticks of dynamite failed to destroy a single structure.[10] Today, Concrete City is used for distinctly uncivilized inhabitation. Once a workers' village, it is now a paintball battlefield, creating a 3-D canvas for simulated violence and suggesting a subtler expressive and chaotic strategy than explosives for breaking down the idea of the model town.

Anti-Urban(e)

While it was the site of innovation and invention, the modern indus-trial city also assaulted the senses, polluted the environment, and, for some, represented the concentrated locus of political and economic oppression. Suspicion arose about the city's customs and mores, often attributed to severing people's fundamental and "natural" relationship to the countryside and self-sustaining agriculture. Following the premise of Howard's diagram, many of modernism's attenuated or diffuse urbanisms—Frank Lloyd Wright's Broadacre City, the Soviet disurbanist plans, and Ludwig Hilberseimer's suburbanization of Chicago—never reconstituted a dense core, while remaining political, revolutionary, *and* architectural. They recognized that new forms of transportation and energy might allow the city to be redefined by temporal rather than spatial dimension.[11] Wright depicted an agrarian refuse from the hoarding, predatory tendencies of Wall Street; the Soviets willfully disaggregated the bourgeois urban power centers; Hilberseimer projected the thinning fabric of the decaying nineteenth-century industrial city.

Characteristically, such revolutionary projects required that the orders of the corrupted "Noble City" be abandoned, opening up a conceptual space between functional determinism and the moribund Serlian signifiers. Despite a lack of density, the schemes remain urban because of the development of networks—the interstate highway and rural electrification, for Wright; rail and air travel, for the Soviets; and the development of decentralized manufacturing, for Hilberseimer. In each case, a reimagined individual found asylum from the formerly urban(e) in new collectives—Wright's small-town agrarian democracy, the Soviets' social condensers, or Hilberseimer's suburban culs-de-sac. Rather than succumbing to the unstructured and often dehumanizing operations of contemporary metropolitanism, they projected synthetic and meaningful social practices and formal languages freed of the constraints of the previous regime. The urban(e) is reconstituted in Wright's formalized warp and weft of a new organic architecture, in the Soviets' fulfillment of earlier formal experiments registered against the aspirations of a proletariat state, and in Hilberseimer's underlying faith in scientific, bureaucratic management.

The utopian aspirations of these attenuated urbanisms remain subject to Michel de Certeau's critique of the "Concept-city," which he defines as an operation that produces its own space unpolluted by the past, a synchronic system that contrasts to tradition, and a universal subject.[12] The Concept-city has no interference with contradictory spatial or political logics. Its relative abstraction, a product of the monetization of all things in its governing system, enabled it to marshal massive sums of capital. This ability to exchange buildings, programs, and even urban subjects within its gridded framework transformed the Concept-city into a version of the Comic City of the marketplace. The inherent mutability of the pieces occupying the grid supported capitalism's apparent requirement to eliminate the strict logic of *any* plan. Ultimately the result is the breakdown of discrete linguistic models. Wright, for example, who opposed the Neoplatonic values inherent to any singular concept, still proposed the family and the one-acre farm as the structural unit of formal and political control and even went so far as to turn money in Broadacre into a temporally restricted commodity in order to counter the destructive forces of capitalism.[13] However, the legacy of Broadacre's liberal individualism can be found in the horizontal urbanism of the vast American commercial landscape.

In previous periods the pits of the coal mines were the energy source that drove urbanization. The valley, like other Rust Belt sites that once fueled the city, would only be formerly urban if it fell outside the broader Concept-city's values. It would be made up of those things that cannot be exchanged within the urbanizing system. At first impression this would be the case. But if, in Howard's inclusive conceptual taxonomy, the inebriated and the insane are relegated to the undifferentiated gaps of the network, his polycentric model seems outdated with the loss of distinction between city and country. The entropic nature of today's urban systems of warehouses, big-box retail, landscapes of waste, and low-density residential suburban growth is all-inclusive. While the pits of the Wyoming Valley produced the piles of many regional cities, today the leveling of difference—the entropic forces unleashed on both landscape and architectural form—necessitates new tools for understanding the postindustrial land pattern.

Though nonsites like the mining properties have a physical presence, their morphologies—their forms—are situated outside conventional norms of both the visible (what can be seen) and the articulate (what can be named). This had banished them from the discussion of their form. Characteristic materials of the nonsite once understood as by-products of the city—like pits and piles, caterings and tailings, detritus and discards—resemble the spatial logic of the preconceptualized past. The intricate relationships of these substances—the earthiness of buildings, land, roads, nature, animals, and humans—bound together and enfolded, resemble Serlio's Satyric City. Like the Satyric City, these nonsites can appear traditional, because their waste materials cannot be sorted, separated, translated, or readily exchanged. These Satyric nonsites quite often are where the objects in its scene are now piled up and pitted, falling back into a second nature of decay.

Fig. 7. Barry Le Va, *By Four Equal Quantities (within four equal spaces:) arranged, rearranged, borrowed, exchanged*, 1967

The Concept-city suppressed waste within its pure visual order, dissembling the excesses of the "metropolis" and its entropic symptoms in the rational forms of the "city." But modernism, in itself, does not necessarily sanction the concept that drives modern architecture's urban(e) form. Mies, for example, despite the ubiquitous use of the grid, never posited a utopia. Instead, his architecture opens up new spatial and linguistic territory within the city. This establishment of a *terrain vague*— the space of the possible—marks the annihilation of urban(e) form. Alan Berger has gone so far as to suggest that these "drosscapes," the waste sites of the city, are not only necessary to the city, but, as with the *terrain vague*, they function as the potential areas of future forms of urbanization.[14] To move beyond this architectural impasse, we have to consider the open formal and political possibilities in today's non-Concept-cities.

A Mine of Inform(e)ation

We do not have to look far to imagine what the form is of a city without a concept. In our present reality the city has disappeared and been replaced by a ubiquitous urbanism. The formless horizontal expanse of sprawl and other wastelands is our political reality. In analyzing its formal qualities, one cannot avoid the obvious correspondence of the valley's landscape to Robert Smithson's world of slag heaps, pours, and rubble mounds. Post-Minimalist work, like the valley's landscape, was distinctly contingent, marginal, temporal, and nonlinguistic, or inform(e)al, especially in its specific choice of materials: Alan Saret's stains and snarls and tangles of electric wire; Robert Morris's piles of detritus; Eva Hesse's slumping, fugitive resin casts that fail to reproduce their molds; and Barry Le Va's free-form orchestration of felt cast-offs and individuated parts, like ball bearings, lead punches, paper towel rolls, and glass shards (fig. 7). As Rosalind Krauss remarked, Smithson exhibited a "formalism redeemed at the expense of modernism."[15]

The critical writing that accompanied the work courted both the nonsensical and performative aspects of language as a complement to its formal excesses.[16] Smithson's world oscillated between "junk" and "text." Krauss remarked that Smithson and others imagined a world that eradicated "those distances that regulate the grid of oppositions, or differences, necessary to the production of meaning."[17] But if satyr was once synonymous with the pastoral, Smithson's terminology, similar to that of Gilles Deleuze and Félix Guattari, was geological. He referred to a new "tectonic" that outlined processes of "sedimentation," "sorting," and consolidation to establish a "thermodynamic" logic of shifting forms and material processes. While architectural techniques of collage may have circumvented the tabula rasa of modernism, they tended to reference the past, maintaining the privileged vantage point of the plan as a strategic tool and the elevation as an indicator of identity. Reverting to near Serlian logic, architects patched together quotations of discarded memes as new linguistic urban and architectural assemblages, so that the city could be read like a concrete text. For the more conservative strains of postmodern architecture, the ubiquitous and banal sameness of the contemporary city was the problem, not, as it was for Smithson, the place of potential.

Smithson, however, was preoccupied with a different understanding of time, and his event structures were simultaneously prehistoric and dystopian/futuristic. In his films, in particular, he uses the conceptual and postindustrial landscape to destabilize identities, fixed locations, and sequential or linear notions of time. Smithson's literary and literal landscapes could not be read, but they could be experienced. "At any rate, the 'pastoral,' it seems, is outmoded," Smithson wrote. "The gardens of history are being replaced by sites of time."[18] He continued:

> By excluding technological processes from the making of art, we began to discover other processes of a more fundamental order. The breakup or fragmentation of matter makes one aware of the sub-strata of the Earth before it is overly refined by industry into sheet metal, extruded I-beams, aluminum channels, tubes, wire, pipe, cold rolled steel, iron bars, etc.... Like the refined "paints" of the studio, the refined "metals" of the laboratory exist within an "ideal system." Such enclosed "pure" systems make it impossible

to perceive any other kinds of processes other than the one of differentiated technology....Refinement of matter from one state to another does not mean that so-called "impurities" of sediment are "bad"—the earth is built on sedimentation and disruption....The fact remains that the mind and things of certain artists are not "unities," but things in a state of arrested disruption....The refuse between mind and matter is a mine of information.[19]

Smithson's fascination with the nonsites of waste and decay countered modernism's "purity" and postmodernism's timeless "gardens of history." Site and the nonsite were shown to be dialectically dependent, not only as they constituted a network of production, but also as they served as dipoles in entropic information systems. In the process of differentiation and identity, the architecture of the modern city was constituted with the nonsite as its other. By transporting sites abandoned in the processes of modernization into the gallery, Smithson effectively reurbanized the nonsite, establishing its role as a terminal node in the urban and linguistic network: the nonsite effectively is the limit of thought and language and, by inference, the city as a concept. In Smithson's estimation, entropic processes threatened to collapse modernism's comic monuments. He depicts Madison Avenue's glass boxes, home to advertising and other "mad men," not as strong silent types but as pathetic and comic figures—the dialectic entropic crystal twins to New Jersey's pitted wasteland. These buildings had also become accumulations of forms *and* words, "heaps of language," piles of information emitting no signal, full of noise, overcome by static. In embracing the waning of form, Smithson's writing verged on a chant: "Literal usage becomes incantatory when all metaphors are suppressed."[20] By exposing and collapsing the temporal and spatial project of modernism, Smithson's critical project threatened to tear down the walls and taboos of linguistic and spatial difference into an entropic gray matter (i.e., thought) that reduced the urban(e) into a provocative and ineffable wasteland. It would be the architect's ambition to tease out form from the virtual situations of the site. Redeeming formalism in architecture subjected to the effects of an entropic urbanism would necessitate engagement with the formless qualities of non-Concepts.

Satyric Urbanism
Modern architecture's attenuated urban concepts were still utopian and pastoral, characterized by proper spacing and organization, and were predicated on either mythical or synchronic notions of time.

However, like Smithson's entropic landscapes, the Satyric traits that distinguish the non-Concept-city stretch urban form to the point of disconnect or collapse. Meaning is effectively eradicated, while the delirium of metropolitan affects can be enhanced. Wittgenstein's early writing and Mies's architecture were predicated on a purposeful silence. Modernism's charged voids were possible only with the expenditure of vast resources of infrastructure, energy, and information.[21] Satyric architecture's *terrain vague*, like the current urban landscape, pauses, hesitates, stutters, and rants. Nonsense and noise, which characterize this architecture, operate at the limits of comprehension and articulation. To be more specific, within the more recent history, moments within these temporal landscapes that appear as "architecture" are the product of weak signals (No-Stop City), tangles of infrastructure (the Sea Terminal at Zeebrugge and the Congrexpo at Lille), or the piling up of excessive information (the Zentrum für Kunst und Medientechnologie at Karlsruhe and the OMA library projects), rather than pure representations of political ideologies. Satyric proposals like these are symptoms rather than cures of cultural forces and, therefore, are politically ambiguous, while suggesting new urban subjects and temporal identities.

For our proposals Satyric architecture exists at the limits of "good form," reproducing the delirium of the metropolis (as opposed to the nobility of the city). Building forms appear as piles of material, arbitrarily tacked and nominally contained. We subscribe to Koolhaas's statement to ignore the problem of the "new" in favor of the "more" and the "modified."[22]

Intensity Not Density

The Socratic question "What is urbanism?" solicits extensive description—urbanism is x and is defined by these quantities. For the New Urbanists, this can be a fairly simple formula of naming ("hamlet"), measuring and setting standards (three people per acre), cutting out samples from history (contextual types), and pasting these nominal forms back into the voids of the urban grid.[23] The dead signals of New Urbanist transects, incorporated into national standards, seek to codify the network in radiating densities from city to town to hamlet, effectively reestablishing Howard's greenbelt logic and appealing to "timeless" values. But their lack of an urbanizing system beyond simplistic marketing trends renders them, at best, idealistic and moralistic pastoralists.

Fig. 8. Gerhard Richter, *Townscape Madrid,* 1968

Despite an apparent lack of density, in many ways the formerly urban would be an impossibility. Everything is urban. If our present condition of sprawl seems to be generated outside pure human agency, it is because the forces that form it are illusive, dynamic, and excessive and can overwhelm any sense of subjective control or agency. We have seen these artifacts, as Paul Virilio notes, in the surrender of the village center to parking lots, where exchange supplants the social bond of the domestic scene and where goods that we do not need pile up in our warehouses.[24] Here architecture is pushed to its limits. "The limit can, therefore, only be drawn in language and what lies on the other side of the limit will be simply nonsense."[25] Intensity, as opposed to the extensive criteria of density, is characterized by qualitative differences of relational elements in process or flux. Extensive entities must emerge fully formed; an intensive urbanism is in the process of becoming. It is the formless and temporal qualities of the "drosscape" that allow for speculation on its future urban potential. In demonstrating a framework for the valley, we have to strategically phase development logistics to keep possibilities open. Questions like "Where is urbanism?" "When is urbanism?" and "How is urbanism?" support the idea of an intensive rather than an extensive moment in processes that structure form.[26] The architecture of these phase-shifting landscapes will be the Satyric articulations within the urban network, the markers, terminals, and relays within an emergent formal language.

Theorems and Non-Concepts for After Urbanisms

Urbanizing Luzerne County's coal towns both demonstrates and requires an intensive phase transition. This might eventually engender an extensive new space whose scale would engage both the nebulous political territory of a displaced and fugitive populace and the defensive enclaves of lifestyle centers, retirement villages, and temporal institutional havens. The project will appear Satyric to the formerly urban(e). The form this space takes will entail sometimes contradictory nonconcepts to consider, four of which I outline here. These nonconcepts are culled from the formal agenda of the art world in order to provide visual accompaniment and also mirrored by latent development in more attenuated urban situations.

Cumulative model: Accumulation of like forms (brushstrokes or buildings) produces local order (recognizable urbanlike clusters) that accumulate toward facsimiles of "city" without any overall order or governing concept other than proximity. Specific materials (ball bearings, plant material, monads, shanties, greenhouses), when set adrift, find local order through their material properties and local forces. The cumulative model is both a time-based notion of a city and a simulation of a city (fig. 8).

Temporal landscape: Mechanical and unauthorized accumulation of material and forces (paint, plant matter, heat, and other raw material that fills the duller expanses of landscapes and warehouses that supply the old city) results in lush fields of time-sensitive effects.

Borrowed orders: Random acts can be temporally sorted and ordered through overlays of borrowed concepts (the grid) to impose artificial appearances of order.

Scatters and fields: Distributions, in contrast to clusters, privilege diffusion over compression and simultaneity over sequence. These organizations are comprehended by moving bodies and offer no privileged position or vantage point, resulting in a new conceptualization of public space.

Terminal Architecture

The valley is, as Smithson might have put it, the site of a terminal architecture of logical contradictions—the place where formal language confronts its limits. It is a crazy quilt of enclaves with no unifying image, political vision, or operative network, but also a node in a national distribution network. The rugged geography of mountains and valleys that hindered westward expansion now causes telecommunication dead zones, but the valley is an important point of information distribution. The Earth Conservancy, having control of large tracts of land in the valley, is in the odd but fortuitous position of replicating the political power of the mining companies, but it lacks the financial resources that might give it political control to implement a sociopolitical structure. Instead it must be opportunistic, using funding from one project as a start-up for the next. The valley is a ruin and an active center; a nonsite and, potentially, a rurally integrated small-town economy; a regional hub and a wasteland; the former energy supplier to early industrial America and a potential money pit of compromised, dormant sites.

Rather than following Hazleton's model of selling to big-box warehouses, which eat up vast areas of land but create few high-paying jobs, the Earth Conservancy courts companies that offer better long-term economic prospects. These big-box commercial headquarters within the properties, temporal social condensers, could act as transdermal patches to alter the valley body politic. The commercial complexes' daytime populations are comparable to those of the patch towns. In these "conceptual Scrantons," as depicted in *The Office,* work in the postindustrial economy is to be avoided; social networking and office politics are the main activity. Commercial enclaves are temporal communities, sites for intensive urban shape, accumulations or singularities within the valley's cultural framework. Other dense cores of residential and commercial concentration are sites for Satyric solutions, providing the best aspect of in-town living with easy access to regional green and blue networks. These patches are also likely to be focused on temporal alternative "lifestyle" centers that are preproductive (college students and village life), semiproductive (commercial distribution centers), and postproductive (assisted living centers, retirement communities). We imagine scattering these non-Concept-cities, contained but irregular enclaves, to provide heterogeneous development at commercial scale, transforming suburban homogeneity toward a wilder nature.

Interruptions and Seams
It is said that in Luzerne County a person could walk underground 15 miles from south to north, from Nanticoke to Pittston, without ever

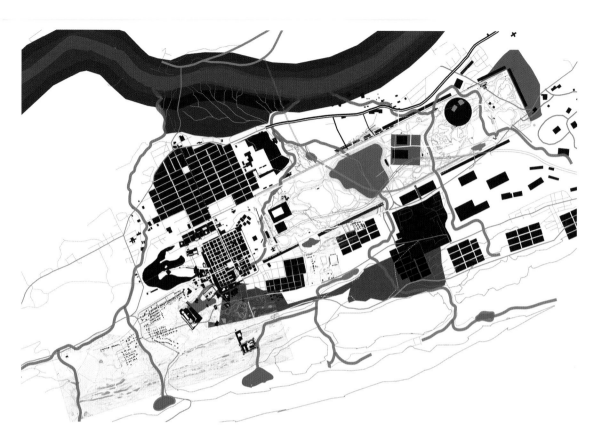

Fig. 9. Earth Conservancy
framework plan

leaving a mine.[27] The subterranean valley is a maze of infinite digressions,
an accidental Mundaneum of disaster. The networks that once bound
the patches together now unravel the valley's social structure. During the
1959 Knox Mine disaster, the Susquehanna River pushed through the roof
of the Ewen Colliery River Slope near Port Griffith, resulting in twelve
deaths and sealing the end of deep mining in eastern Pennsylvania.

The western half of the valley is stagnant. Open pits interrupt natural
watercourses that originate in reservoirs in the high southern ridge and
run to the Susquehanna River, eventually emptying into the Delaware
Water Gap, thus affecting a major portion of the Mid-Atlantic states.
While the area may not always be a pile, it is certainly a socioeconomic
pit that mirrors the historic stock value of the region's coal companies. When operating, the deeper the pit the higher the value to the city
proper; now, however, those same pits are moribund zones of activity,
holes in the valley fabric. In our proposal, supported by studies from
the Army Corps of Engineers, we recommend repairing the streambed
system and extending the wetlands buffer zone to 500 feet, improving

Fig. 10. Perspective
of the Thinkbelt

these vital resources' future ecology while also increasing real estate value for abutting properties. New trails and networks may be the only way to bring the valley back to its senses. "Just as we cannot think of spatial objects at all apart from space, or temporal objects apart from time, so we cannot think of any object apart from the possibility of its connection with other things."[28]

Trolleys were once the nervous system of the valley, running down Hanover and Middle roads to give mobility to miners as they shifted from pit to pit. The proposed infrastructure replacement, the concrete stent of the South Valley Parkway, seems absurd when the idea of a fixed body is beyond its statistical lifespan. As shown in the Mine Fire Greenhouse Project, we imagine more nimble infrastructures. Redeploying mass transit on these roads will be like applying shock therapy, reanimating the moribund urban system and giving mobility to those without access to cars. In the Mine Fire Greenhouse Project we show that the labyrinths of the valley are its future circuitry. Further-more, our proposed trail system will make north–south traversal of the

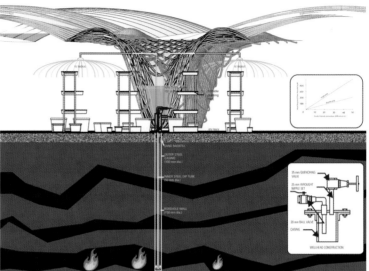

Above: Fig. 11. Mine Fire
Greenhouse grid-shell canopy

Right, top: Fig. 12. Mine Fire
Greenhouse grid-shell canopy and
taproot heat-circulation system

Right, bottom: Fig. 13. Mine Fire
Greenhouse program diagram

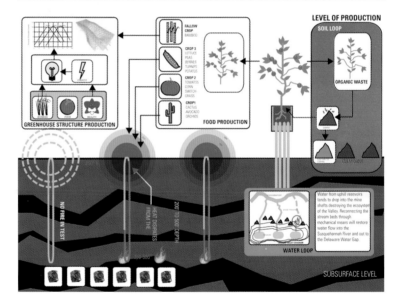

valley accessible for bicycles and pedestrians, interconnecting town centers and school properties. Out-of-service freight lines along the Susquehanna could be used for future commuter rail service. Extending commuter rail service from New York to nearby Scranton to regenerate the "Electric City" is under discussion.

The Thinkbelt

The contiguous Earth Conservancy properties running from the Wyoming Valley Country Club to the Luzerne County Community College are as large as New York's Central Park (fig. 9). Central Park is an aesthetic enhancement and a civic utility of reservoirs, public spaces, and institutions. Our Thinkbelt, named in homage to Cedric Price, would physically connect several educational institutions—Luzerne County Community College, Misericordia University, Penn State's Wilkes-Barre branch campus, King's College, and the local public schools—into a supercampus (fig. 10). These institutions are training local residents for jobs in the distribution and service economy, like trucking, health care, and green-energy technology.[29]

While the patches of towns in Luzerne County are rooted in the valley's traditions, the Thinkbelt is progressive, an opportunity for a new idea of the office park with typologies that use intelligent and sustainable landscape design. The Thinkbelt will function as the valley's employment core and as a regional incubator for green redevelopment concepts—integrating new storm-water and land practices, renewable energy, and economic development strategies, which can be tested and developed by local universities.

Several schemes were shown to visualize the potential political aspirations of the plan. The linear scheme, which connects directly to the main roads, is laissez-faire, with limitations determined solely by topography; the void scheme with large private housing developments is a form of a City Beautiful agenda without grand civic nostalgia; the raked void scheme gives symbolic power to the former mining operations. It captures both the sublime qualities of parking lots and toxic-land management and the benefits of the enclaves of superpatches. Development is encouraged not only at the Thinkbelt's borders, but also within it. Design covenants are voluntary for an alternative urbanism and will insure inventive land-use policies but not dictate aesthetics, while recognizing that the building's image is tied to its performance in the landscape. Temporary and mobile architectures might adapt to the needs and capacities of the regional education system. The Thinkbelt might function as both a corporate office park and a regional and cultural landscape attraction.

Fig. 14. Mine Fire Greenhouse perspective

Afterburn

In 1915 a miner left a lit carbide lamp in the Red Ash Coal Mine in Laurel Run, Pennsylvania, causing a fire that burns to this day. The area of the fire is in the south limb of the Wilkes-Barre synclinorium, which is 4 miles wide and runs northeast–southwest along the southern ridge of Luzerne Valley. The coal deposits in this area run in three layers—the Ross, Bottom, and Top Red Ash. Man-made barriers constructed in the 1920s and the natural anthracite coal deposits that bound the control area prevent the spread of the fire. In 1967, when Interstate 81 was constructed, further efforts were made to control the fire in order to prevent collapses of the road system.

Anthracite's density makes it difficult to ignite, and it took several decades to discover how to use it as an energy source for the early Industrial Revolution. Fissures in coal allow for the transfer of energy, and consequently fractures in the natural bed formations allow areas to burn when oxygen infiltrates the beds. Fires that have been burning under nearby Centralia since 1962 reach temperatures of over 1,400 degrees Fahrenheit and have caused massive environmental and economic damage, but the less extreme Laurel Run fires reach temperatures in the range of 120 to 150 degrees Fahrenheit at the surface. The introduction of oxygen can increase those temperatures to make direct-source heating or power generation possible, but they could also jeopardize nearby communities, including Wilkes-Barre, and risk structurally compromising Interstate 80.

Historical maps of Laurel Run, supplied by engineers associated with the Pennsylvania Bureau of Mining and Reclamation, suggest that approximately 50 percent of the original coal resources remain. This would indicate that the potential fuel supply would last well beyond any foreseeable standard for sustainable use; however, inspections over the years show that the fire's movement is unpredictable. While the fire should burn up the slope of the hill, as a ground fire would, the erratic fissures in the bed's formation mean that the fire jumps unpredictably. To inventively remediate the property, Komanda's Mine Fire Greenhouse Project requires drilling geothermal wells at 500-foot intervals, working inward at hot spots, and tracing subgrade heat sources by a structure that extends along these erratic source points. At live fire sources, a closed-loop pipe system is inserted into the shaft to heat water (fig. 11).

The dangers of producing local heat-energy sources mitigate any plans for an energy plant. In addition, the site's volatile ground conditions

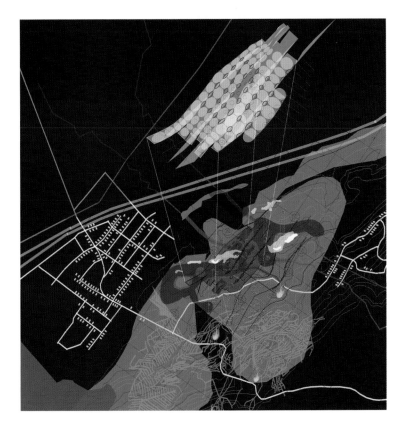

Fig. 15. Mine Fire Greenhouse plan

are unsafe for standard redevelopment scenarios. Because the Earth Conservancy hopes to utilize its Laurel Run property, we project its best use as a new public garden and conservatory. The free heat source will extend growing seasons and make the proposition commercially feasible. However, the unpredictable nature of the source requires a transportable lightweight structure to capture the heat. To accomplish this, we propose a hyperparabolic bamboo grid shell, whose structural materials can be grown and harvested on-site (fig. 12). The grid shells will be covered with a 6-milliliter layer of either polyvinyl or sustainable polylimonene carbonates. Organic waste from the horticulture operation will be used to rehabilitate the property's compromised soils.

The Mine Fire Greenhouse Project is a bootstrapping operation (fig. 13). Along with the bamboo on-site food and rare plant specimens will be grown. Convenient access to the interstate allows for these plants to be distributed easily and for tourists to get to the site. The spectacle of extreme agriculture, the billowing steam clouds of the coal-burning heat vents, and the potential for spas and passive recreation could make this former disaster zone into a regional attraction. Other plans include extending the Earth Conservancy's regional mulching program on-site and establishing experimental gardens for biofuel.

The Mine Fire Greenhouse Project has no real dominant geometric order. Instead it is structured by larger physical and economic systems, which have little presence in the visible spectrum. It is a park-scape that is self-generative and distinctly nonhumanist. However, the expressive structure of its bamboo grid shell will turn a negative image of the valley's industrial past into a positive image for its future (figs. 14, 15). It is our hope that with this project we not only rehabilitate the valley's image but also develop a public infrastructure that is progressive and generative of new publics.

---

1   Rem Koolhaas, "Nevada," in Rem Koolhaas and Bruce Mau, *S,M,L,XL* (New York: Monacelli Press, 1995), 201.

2   Duane D. Braun, *Surficial Geology of the Nanticoke 7.5-Minute Quadrangle, Luzerne County, Pennsylvania* (Harrisburg, Pa.: Pennsylvania Geological Survey, 2008).

3   H. C. Bradsby, ed., *History of Luzerne County Pennsylvania* (Chicago: S. B. Nelson & Co., 1893), 12, http://www.usgwarchives.org/pa/luzerne/1893hist.

4   Ibid., 12.

5   Geoffrey Wolf, *The Art of Burning Bridges* (New York: Knopf, 2003), 4.

6   Braun, *Surficial Geology of the Nanticoke 7.5-Minute Quadrangle*, 24.

7   David Grahame Shane, *Recombinant Urbanism: Conceptual Modeling in Architecture, Urban Design and City Theory* (London: Wiley-Academy, 2005), 19. This atomistic notion of language was criticized by Ludwig Wittgenstein in the *Philosophical Investigations*, where he summarizes Saint Augustine's philosophy of language from *The City of God*: "The individual words in language name objects—sentences are combinations of such names. In this picture of language we find the roots of the following idea: Every word has a meaning. This meaning is correlated with the word. It is the object for which the word stands."

8   Shane, *Recombinant Urbanism*, 27.

9   To this extent, the nomenclature of urbanism is still retained by the New Urbanists's transect system and other standard measures for sustainable growth, such as the LEED smart growth principles.

10   "The Concrete City," http://home.comcast.net/~tecsite/ConcreteCity/Concrete.html.

11   Jonathan Hughes and Simon Sadler, *Non-Plan: Essays on Freedom, Participation and Change in Modern Architecture and Urbanism* (Oxford: Architectural Press, 2000). The editors of *New Society* (Peter Hall, Paul Barker, Reyner Banham, and Cedric Price), Archizoom, and later OMA might also be included in this list, but they represent a different ideological paradigm.

12   Michel de Certeau, *The Practice of Everyday Life* (Berkeley and Los Angeles: University of California Press, 1984), 94.

13   Wright's Broadacre City, like other earlier utopian projections, saw monetization as the cause of the demise of fundamental Jeffersonian values. In more extreme cases of utopian projection, like William Dean Howells's novel *A Traveler from Altruria*, money itself is rejected.

14   Alan Berger, *Drosscape; Wasting Land in Urban America* (New York: Princeton Architectural Press, 2006), 18–33.

15   Thierry de Duve, "The Monochrome and the Blank Canvas," in *Kant After Duchamp* (Cambridge, Mass.: MIT Press, 1996), 261.

16   See Rosalind Krauss, "Sense and Sensibility: Reflections on Post-Modern Sculpture," *Artforum*, November 1973, 43–53.

17   Rosalind Krauss, "A User's Guide to Entropy," in Yve-Alain Bois and Rosalind Krauss, *L'Informe: Mode d'Emploi* (Paris: Centre Georges Pompidou, 1996).

18   Robert Smithson, "The Sedimentation of the Mind: Earth Projects," in *The Writings of Robert Smithson*, ed. Nancy Holt (New York: New York University Press, 1979), 86.

19   Ibid., 87.

20   Smithson, "Press Release Language to Be Looked at and/or Things to be Read," in *The Writings of Robert Smithson*, 104.

21   For example, he lists the alternative forms of matter that could have been made from the materials used for the Congress Expo Hall at Lille. See Koolhaas and Mau, *S,M,L,XL*.

22   Ibid.

23   This practice of cutting and pasting historically identifiable transects or urban set pieces is often shared by landscape urbanist projects, which establish standards and practices like urban farming as an aesthetic and moral obligation rather than an outcome of material processes. At the "Formerly Urban" conference, Charles Waldheim noted that the term "landscape" was originally aesthetic, describing "an expanse of scenery" rather than a process.

24   Paul Virilio, *The Futurism of the Instant* (Cambridge, U.K.: Polity Press, 2010), 64–65.

25   Ludwig Wittgenstein, "Preface," in *Tractatus Logico-Philosophicus* (Mineola, N.Y.: Dover Publications), 27.

26   "Gilles Deleuze," *The Stanford Encyclopedia of Philosophy* (Fall 2008 edition), http://plato.stanford.edu/archives/fall2008/entries/deleuze/. Accessed June 15, 2011.

27   Edward F. Hanlon, *The Wyoming Valley: An American Portrait* (Wilkes-Barre, Pa.: Winsor, 1983), 56–57.

28   Wittgenstein, "Preface," 30.

29   Cedric Price's concerns for the role of education in similar economic circumstances echo the broader goals of the community college system. He writes, "Education is today little more than a method of distorting the individual's [mind and behavior] to enable him to benefit from existing social and economic patterning. Such an activity benevolently controlled and directed by an elite can do little more than improve the range and network of structures it already has under its control." See Stanley Mathews, *From Agit-Prop to Free Space: The Architecture of Cedric Price* (London: Black Dog Publishing, 2007), 198–99.

Landscape's M.O.
Julia Czerniak

AUTOMOTIVE

FLINT
POP 124,943
METRO 443,883
2000 CENSUS POPULATION

DETROIT
POP 910,920
METRO 4,403,437
2009 CENSUS POPULATION

TOLEDO
POP 316,851
METRO 650,955
2007 CENSUS POPULATION

CLEVELAND
POP 431,639
METRO 2,250,871
2009 CENSUS POPULATION

METALS

YOUNGSTOW
POP 72,925
METRO 570,7
2008 CENSUS POPUL

COLUMBUS
POP 754,885
METRO 1,773,120
2008 CENSUS POPULATION

DAYTON
POP 166,179
METRO 848,153
2000 CENSUS POPULATION

CINCINNATI
POP 333,013
METRO 2,155,137
2009 CENSUS POPULATION

Copyright 2005 - geology.com

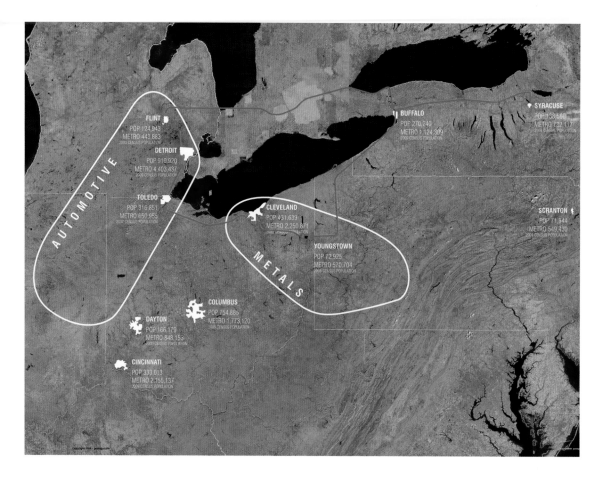

The following labels appear on the map:

FLINT
POP 124,943
METRO 443,883
2000 CENSUS POPULATION

DETROIT
POP 910,920
METRO 4,403,437
2009 CENSUS POPULATION

TOLEDO
POP 316,851
METRO 650,955
2007 CENSUS POPULATION

BUFFALO
POP 270,240
METRO 1,124,309
2009 CENSUS POPULATION

SYRACUSE
POP 138,160
METRO 732,117
2009 CENSUS POPULATION

CLEVELAND
POP 431,639
METRO 2,250,871
2009 CENSUS POPULATION

YOUNGSTOWN
POP 72,925
METRO 570,704
2009 CENSUS POPULATION

SCRANTON
POP 71,944
METRO 549,430
2009 CENSUS POPULATION

COLUMBUS
POP 754,885
METRO 1,773,120
2009 CENSUS POPULATION

DAYTON
POP 166,179
METRO 848,153
2009 CENSUS POPULATION

CINCINNATI
POP 333,013
METRO 2,155,137
2009 CENSUS POPULATION

AUTOMOTIVE

METALS

Fig. 1. Route of Rust Belt tour

In late summer 2010 I spent a week driving around the Rust Belt region of the United States. My aim was simple—leave from Syracuse, New York, make a loop around Lake Ontario, and visit four cities: Youngstown, Cleveland, Detroit, and Flint (fig. 1). These cities are tidily paired and offer remnants of their specific pasts. Youngstown and Cleveland, Ohio, a small and a large city 75 miles apart, are both in what was the center of a steel-producing region; Detroit and Flint, Michigan, 68 miles apart, also a large and a small city, are both in what was the center of the automotive industry. All of these cities have lost significant population since 1950, and their struggles with the implications of this loss are readily visible.

My perception of these cities was previously formed through maps, images, or short visits, and my knowledge of them through projects and media. Here, however, my aim was to look beyond the way these cities are popularly characterized by their loss of population and

Downtown Youngstown

subsequent disinvestment—and associated images of crumbling
infrastructure, decay, and obsolescence—and witness how landscape
in such places operates when left to its own logic. That is, how does
landscape appear and perform when not constrained by maintenance
and management—muscled instead by ecological, socioeconomic,
and political forces? In these circumstances landscape's M.O., its
modus operandi or "method of operating," is clearer. In its messiness,
messages, and mediums, there are clues for the potential of landscape
design to address the formerly urban city across many scales.

Fig. 2. Vacant land (in gray)
and topography overlaid,
Youngstown, Ohio

The intent of this essay is to share photographs and drawings from
my wanderings, each of whose subtle logic offers possible directions
for design work. In some cases these directions unfold by reinforcing
what is currently being done in the design disciplines, in others, by the
new roles we give landscape through our disciplinary and professional
efforts. In all cases my views from the ground have formed the basis
of a set of future possibilities for these and other formerly urban cities.

Ground

In the visionary plan of Youngstown that Hunter Morrison compre-
hensively discusses in "Lessons Learned from a Shrinking City" in
this book, the logics of landscape—in this case the hydric condition
of the ground—drives a component of a thoughtful shrinking strategy
for the city. This both reflects upon and corrects poor decisions hastily
made when the city was quickly growing and industry was thriving. For

Fig. 3. New streetscapes and event surfaces, downtown Youngstown, Ohio

example, housing for African American steelworkers was built cheaply and quickly on the east side of Youngstown in land considered a swamp. The nature of the ground was of no import.[1] Today, the dampness of this low-lying area—suggested by lush planting and visibly rotting building materials—coupled with years of neglect since the steel industry left, has made it one of the most unstable neighborhoods in the city (fig. 2). The 2010 plan recognizes that poorly drained land is not optimal for redevelopment, and that it is better to group it with similar types of land into a larger parcel. By renaming and remaking the culturally pejorative "swamp" into a future "wetland," the plan repositions the area's hydric

UNIVERSITY CIRCLE

DOWNTOWN

soils as an asset within the larger area. Here the landscape becomes
a subject in its own right, a thriving performative ground, rather than
a background for building.[2] Other cities are using the nature of the
ground in similar ways to guide their planning efforts. The practice is
arguably valuable in projecting urban futures.

Planner Terry Schwartz and the Cleveland Urban Design Collaborative
use characteristics of Cleveland's largely vacant ground plane—
including its hydrologic soil groups, riparian and headwater systems,
and surface porosity—to guide citywide strategies for the reuse of
vacant land. This strategy was so logical and convincing that it was
adopted by the Cleveland City Planning Commission.[3]

Image

Driving from the periphery of Youngstown into its small, gridded downtown, nestled along the Mahoning River industrial corridor, I quickly
saw that decisions have been made to shore up its appearance. Well-
traveled entry roads and important city streets have been enhanced
with new street lights, carefully screened parking, and lushly planted
traffic islands that collect and cleanse storm water, while other streets
languish.[4] The appearance of these new streetscapes is shored up by the
entrepreneurial companies indexed along them, such as those promised through the Youngstown Business Incubator. The locally famous
start-up company Turning Technologies has stayed downtown, moving

Fig. 4. The Bus Rapid Transit (BRT)
line along the Euclid Corridor,
Cleveland, Ohio

from their small start-up space in the incubator into 30,000 square feet of new space next door. This suggests the potential of Youngstown as what *Entrepreneurial Magazine* calls "one of the ten best cities in which to start a business."[5]

The potential for urban activities is more subtly apparent in Youngstown's new image (fig. 3). On the riverbank adjacent to downtown, the landscape investment is simple: a sloped plane of grass for people to gather and a vertical surface for projecting information. One can imagine this space filled with people, lawn chairs, picnic baskets, blankets, and umbrellas—conjuring up an image of a busy and vital Youngstown as might be pictured in a photograph by Andreas Gursky, although I did not see this activity during my visit.

What activates this particular space, however, are the efforts to make an event happen: a combination of space where the event can be held, a sponsor to pay for it, and an event that attracts a crowd. Designers are experts at programming the public spaces of the city. Just think of the extensive program lists that accompany most landscape and urban design competitions, such as community gardens, art installations, musical performances, and literary readings. But imagining program is not enough. Designers must think beyond the rather simple question of "what to do" toward the more complex one of "how to get things done."[6] This would require bringing together local not-for-profits, the development community, and the private and public sector as well as those in planning, policy, finance, economics, and real estate development to *facilitate* the event, not just program it.

Infrastructure

A short drive northwest from Youngstown brought me to Cleveland, a city whose population has slowly spiraled from a peak of 900,000 in 1950 to a hundred-year low of 396,815 in 2010.[7] There I saw ways that landscape has been combined with infrastructure in an effort to facilitate change at both city and neighborhood scales.

The Bus Rapid Transit (BRT) along the Euclid Corridor is both a transportation project that connects two commercial hubs of the city—downtown and University Circle, almost seven miles apart—and an urban design project with ambitions to catalyze redevelopment in between these two nodes.[8] The clarity of the transit route, which is literally a line, and the efficiency of the transit design, which includes designated bus lanes, signal prioritization, and a stylized

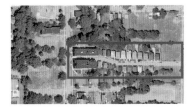

Existing

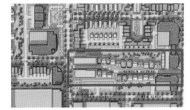

Proposed

Existing

vehicle, enable people to swiftly and efficiently move through this part of the city (fig. 4). The legibility of the system—that is, its capacity to be understood in its intentions, identity, and image—serves an important role. It both enables change (through, for example, increasing the real estate value of land parcels adjacent to its route) and represents it (in other words, standing for change that has yet to appear). Using transit infrastructure as a legible and resilient system can inscribe a framework for the emergence of a new city within the fabric of the old, a strategy that has precedence in other Rust Belt cities, such as in the Connective Corridor in Syracuse.[9]

At a different scale, I saw ways that landscape was combined with infrastructure in two Cleveland neighborhoods to catalyze their revitalization. Both St. Luke's (the redevelopment of a former hospital site) and Upper Chester (near the Cleveland Clinic) are part of the LEED-ND (Leadership in Energy and Environmental Design for Neighborhood Development) pilot project, the U.S. Green Building Council's new program designed to extend the impact of green design from the single building to the wider fabric of the city. LEED-ND ratings are based on many criteria, including the existing potentials and projected development of such things as ease of bicycle, car, and pedestrian connections; promise of compact development; and street

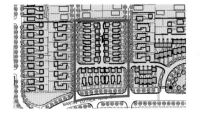

Proposed

Fig. 5. St. Luke's and Upper Chester neighborhoods' commitment to historic density, Cleveland, Ohio

networks that perform environmentally through bio-swales, porous pavements, and curb extensions to manage storm water. Both St. Luke's and Upper Chester have committed to rebuilding their neighborhoods in ways that are compatible with their historic densities, all the while prioritizing green infrastructure and connections to larger networks (fig. 5).[10] It is noteworthy that a full 71 of the 110 possible LEED-ND certification points implicate the landscape rather than some other aspect of design development. In other words, according to LEED-ND, the landscape is the medium through which sustainable cities are made.

Furthermore, the LEED-ND system provides the opportunity to explore what architect and urbanist Mohsen Mostafavi describes in his book *Ecological Urbanism* as the tension between disciplinary knowledge and sustainability. The system takes its ambitions of building responsibly from the object (the building) to the field (the city).[11] In other words, the formerly urban landscape is a fertile site where seemingly antithetical notions of theory and practice play out.

Nature-Scapes

After a few days of driving around Youngstown and Cleveland, the iconic cities of the coal and steel belt, I headed north to Detroit, the poster child of the formerly urban city. Here the possibilities for landscape seem endless. The city demonstrates how landscape is what urbanist James Corner calls a "provisional state of matter on its way to becoming something else."[12] Driving through neighborhood after neighborhood of seemingly disappearing city (out of Detroit's 138-square-mile area, 40 are vacant or foreclosed), I witnessed the residential landscape undergoing ecological succession—the gradual taking over of previously built-up land by plant and animal species. At some point animal populations will reinhabit these former neighborhoods, and although I expected to see raccoons, rabbits, or pheasants at any point, I never did.

It is significant that ecological succession is recognized in the various efforts for planning the city. One visionary group, the Community Development Advocates of Detroit (CDAD), believes that the reinvention of Detroit is based on a unique array of living choices, one of the more provocative being "urban homestead sectors."[13] Here residents can choose to reside in a large home surrounded by a natural landscape, living off the grid while experimenting with alternative energy programs, and pay lower taxes as a result.[14] The group also pictures what they aptly call "nature-scapes," which they describe as "low-maintenance,

1. Traditional Residential Sectors
2. Spacious Residential Transition Zones
3. Urban Homestead Sectors
4. Naturescapes
5. Green Venture Zones
6. Green Thoroughfares
7. Industry Zones
8. Village Hubs
9. Shopping Hubs
10. City Hubs
11. Downtown

managed landscapes intended to bolster air and water quality and
support indigenous wildlife."[15] These seemingly radical choices are
joined by their other more conventional and self-explanatory ones, such
as "green thoroughfares" and "industry zones" (fig. 6).[16] What they all
share, however, is significant in two ways. First, the CDAD imagines a
new Detroit as the first city in the United States to respond to its landscape surplus as an *abundance*.[17] That is, they are not apologetic about
Detroit's emergent landscape, nor are they optimistic that the city's
urbanistic return will be based on previous settlement patterns and,
by extension, density. Second, their planning document is aptly called
a "framework" rather than a "plan," and in this way they propose
"future directions" for sectors that are not specifically located in space.
Not only does this eliminate the wholesale forecasting of the elimination
of neighborhoods (with its political and social risks), but it also allows
future development to be based on the specifics of stakeholder support

Fig. 6. Options for living choices
offered by the Community
Development Advocates of
Detroit (CDAD) juxtaposed with
formerly urban neighborhoods,
Detroit, Michigan

Fig. 7. Successional growth
and its aestheticization,
Detroit, Michigan

for a given area. CDAD's vision for Detroit's future is based on the potential of specific site conditions coupled with strategies for moving these scenarios forward.

Representation

The only work of contemporary landscape design I saw in Detroit was PEG's Mies van der Rohe Plaza near Lafayette Park. This small project (3,300 square feet), located between two buildings in a small shopping plaza, presented itself as a modulated and thickened surface of custom concrete pavers filled with five species of drought-tolerant plants.[18] How this surface resonated with the successional growth apparent in neighborhood sidewalks struck me (fig. 7). That the project aetheticizes—in facts represents—this condition is significant, as it *elevates* what is conventionally considered the image of landscape blight by referring to it in a celebrated outdoor space.

At a time when disciplinary concerns with landscape's performance seem exhausted—or at least it is recognized that landscape's appearance cannot be suppressed—how a landscape looks matters. Landscape is, after all, a system of representation—comprised of words, drawings, pictures, and the landscape medium itself. To suspend landscape's pictorial capacity when imaging new urban modalities and lifestyles seems unfortunate. By re-presenting new exterior landscape forms and images, PEG's plaza is asking users to think differently about what urban spaces do, how they are made, and what they might look like. In so doing they condition our way of seeing and ultimately imaging the landscape—and the future of the city.

After leaving PEG's plaza, I drove by architect Andrew Zago's recently completed project in Detroit Park. The 2,000-square-foot outdoor pavilion is used by the organization Greening of Detroit, a not-for-profit established to "guide and inspire the reforestation of Detroit" as part of a green infrastructure program whose aim is to maximize the environmental health of urban communities.[19] Ironically, although landscape appears everywhere in this city, Detroit lost over half a million trees between 1950 and 1980—during a key period of its shrinkage—due to disease and attrition.[20] According to Zago, the pavilion serves as a shelter for children's classes and for Greening's annual events. I was struck by this new pavilion's appearance, quite different from PEG's work. The structure is made of steel, and the pavilion's canopy is composed of numerous plastic tubes threaded through its upper frame. These tubes not only function as a water management system by collecting and channeling rainwater but also present a radically new image for a pavilion by recalling subsurface urban infrastructure that is here repurposed. Furthermore, the canopy of the pavilion functions like the canopy of a tree by inter-cepting rainfall, a naturalized storm-water management strategy. Here is a project that is highly performative but is not shy about the powerful role of its appearance, an apt example for similar projects in similar contexts.

Space

One of the most powerful and unexpected moments of my tour of Detroit occurred when I was aimlessly driving. I found myself within several spatial conditions that are not easily named, arising not out of the forces of design but those of the economy. One particular space of new typologies and relationships struck me—a leftover space edged by fronts and sides of housing blocks and bisected by sidewalks and their attendant curbs, remnants of previous streets. Historic light fixtures, no doubt marking a particularly significant streetscape now past, defined one edge. In this case the space was completed by my car, producing a sort of ironic Motor City effect (fig. 8). This bizarrely creative landscape cannot be described by the conventional language of landscape archi-tecture. The words we use to define outdoor typologies—park, quad, center, yard, green, plaza—cannot adequately capture its nuances, although they can be loosely associated with many of its elements.

Leftover spaces of the city—spaces that result when large infrastructural changes are made in the urban fabric or when a new highway is built— have intrigued landscape architects and urbanists for quite some time.

Fig. 8. Spatial leftover as new
typology, Detroit, Michigan

Urban landscape projects such as Glass City in Toledo, by Marpillero
Pollak Architects and CLEAR, directly engage such spaces. Glass City
works within the spatial residue of a highway to both produce a memo-
rable gateway into Toledo's Warehouse District and collect and cleanse
storm water as part of its image. What is provocative in this space
I found is how the leftover reads as a primary figure. Many comparable
projects likely exist in similarly decentralized cities. The formerly
urban city is a place from which to imagine new landscape conditions.

Street
While driving through Detroit's neighborhoods it was difficult for
me to overlook the potential of the street. The overgrown vegetation
made it easy to envision the potential of the reforestation programs,
nature-scapes, and green infrastructure systems already mentioned.
But what about the lonely street sign as a reminder of a place's significant history? Street names have two parts: the first, usually individual,
name is referred to as the "specific" (the part of real interest); the second

indicates the type of street, the "generic" (such as boulevard, avenue, drive, or street).[21] The familiar streets and avenues of Detroit—Rosa Parks and Woodward boulevards, even 8 Mile Road (made famous by rapper Eminem)—are easily outnumbered by those whose specific is less familiar. On the corner of McGraw and Wabash streets, not far from Rosa Parks Boulevard, I found a street marker, the only element of street infrastructure remaining on the block. Wabash street recalls, of course, the Wabash Railroad, which operated in the mid-central United States. The history of McGraw Street, however, has long passed from memory.

Designers working in a formerly urban context have the ability to imbue its future with a sense of its past by unpacking the logic of its street names. This is already happening in Syracuse. In the Near Westside neighborhood, a disenfranchised urban community, the north-south streets were all named after Central New York counties (such as Tioga, Oswego, and Seneca), while the east-west streets echoed Central New York towns (Marcellus, Fabius, etc.). As part of the strategy for signage and wayfinding within the neighborhood plan, the designers marked these logics by planting trees with red fall color in one direction, and yellow fall color in the other.[22]

Detroit streets are not only places of meaning but also places of action. One such action is the Formula One race that is hosted in its streets. The event is meant to improve the international image of the Motor City, an automobile reference not lost on its organizers.[23] More provocative are activities that recall and enable the street as a place of activism, where citizens uphold their constitutional rights to free speech and assembly.[24] The phrase "taking it to the streets" has political connotations; citizens can stage public protests in the streets when conventional political channels and processes no longer effect change.[25]

I drove down the streets of artist Tyree Guyton's Heidelberg Project, which he describes as a response to the "cruelty and meanness of the street," his street, and to the selling of crack near the house in which he grew up.[26] His aim was to make something so wonderful that people had to "put their fear aside and come see." Guyton employed the design of an outdoor art environment to improve the lives in his challenged urban neighborhood.[27] A different kind of street art event is Dancing on the Street (DOTS), a festival that celebrates Detroit's diversity through music and food. The highlight of the event has crowds dancing down the street to Michael Jackson's "Thriller" (fig. 9).

Fig. 9. The streets of the Heidelberg
Project, Detroit, Michigan

Land

After a few days in Detroit I headed north to Flint, to the city whose struggles were made famous in producer and director Michael Moore's film *Roger & Me*. I had known about the Genesee County Land Bank and its ability to address poor land use and population decline through buying land on the open market and assembling it into larger parcels. I also knew of its ability to demolish and rehabilitate old structures, or even build new ones.[28] It was on the ground, however, that I first saw the early effects of its policies, where parcels of formerly derelict properties were being joined to adjacent public uses like community gardens and parks.

Perhaps a more interesting example of this land bank's efforts is when it takes on projects that others have given up on. According to a local developer who gave me a brief tour of one such project—the long-unoccupied Durant Hotel in downtown Flint—its redevelopment makes a strong statement to residents and visitors alike that locals will no longer tolerate big empty buildings in their city.[29] In this way the land bank reclaims interior and exterior space, and in doing so produces new places to activate the city (fig. 10).

As designers imagine future potentials for the formerly urban city, land banks could benefit tremendously from their work. As this volume has suggested, revitalizing a shrinking city does not necessarily depend on increasing its land mass or population. Landscape architects can play a key role in planned shrinkage by guiding how it occurs, such as the ways in which land is banked or swapped to achieve the greatest

urban design benefits. Also, designers have the ability to foreground
the idea of "land" in land banking, here understood as (referring to
its Indo-European root) "a collection of people and their relationship
to each other and to the ground they share."[30] Keeping people in mind
when forging emerging policies will insure the highest and best use
for once-vacant property and the promise it holds for future urbanities.

This thousand-mile drive enhanced my perception and conception of
the Rust Belt in unforeseen ways, as well as extended my understanding
of the role that urban landscape design and its associated disciplines
can play in its remaking. To discuss landscape's M.O. then—replete
with its association with police work—is a way to suggest the orderly

Fig. 10. Reclaimed territory of the
land bank, Flint, Michigan

recording and coding of information designed to reveal habits, traits, or practices.[31] Although my itinerary was haphazard, the way landscape appeared and performed was not. In the formerly urban city, landscape's potential was present in all of its richness, and the circumstances in which I observed its traits were consistent. Embedded in these sites are clues that I have just begun to examine, clues that will expand landscape's disciplinary base when projecting urban futures.

1   Provocative discussions of the potentials of the ground and the site include Carol Burns's now-famous essay, "On Site: Architectural Preoccupations," in *Drawing, Building, Text: Essays in Architectural Theory* (New York: Princeton Architectural Press, 1991), 147–67.

2   Elizabeth K. Meyer has, for quite some time, discussed landscape in these terms—not as a "background" for architecture, but as a subject in its own right.

3   See the Cleveland Urban Design Collaborative, http://www.cudc.kent.edu.

4   This practice is enabled by the program Youngstown Cityscape, Revitalizing Downtown Youngstown and Gateways through Beautification, Education and Preservation. See http://youngstowncityscape.com.

5   I saw this fact advertised on a large banner hung on a downtown Youngstown building facade. To read more about this, see Jason Daley, "Where to Be an Entrepreneur," *Entrepreneur*, http://www.entrepreneur.com/article/202666, July 20, 2009.

6   This is part of the mission of UPSTATE: A Center for Design, Research, and Real Estate at the Syracuse University School of Architecture, where I am director.

7   Census Data, 2010, as cited in http://www.cleveland.com/datacentral/index.

8   For a greater discussion on the impact of the Euclid Corridor and Cleveland's future, see McLain Clutter's essay in this volume.

9   This language comes from the competition entry for the Syracuse Connective Corridor by landscape architects and urbanists Field Operations with the local design firm CLEAR.

10   In "Greater Cleveland's Wealth in 'Green' Neighborhood Development" (http://www.gcbl .org/blog/marc-lefkowitz/cleveland-pilots-green-neighborhood-development), Marc Lefkowitz describes the points system as follows: "The project can achieve a variety of points from four separate categories: Smart Location and Linkage, Neighborhood Pattern and Design, Green Construction and Technology, and Innovation and Design." Its primary ambition, he says, is to "improve land-use patterns, neighborhood design, and technology in the United States."

11   See Mohsen Mostafavi, "Why Ecological Urbanism? Why Now?" in *Ecological Urbanism* (Baden, Switzerland: Lars Müller Publishers, 2010).

12   For more on this characteristic of landscape, see James Corner, "Landscape Urbanism," in *Landscape Urbanism: A Manual for the Machinic Landscape*, ed. Mohsen Mostafavi and Ciro Najle (London: Architectural Association, 2003), 58–63.

13   The full title of the planning document referred to here is "Community Development Futures Task Force Neighborhood Revitalization Strategic Framework," prepared by the CDAD (Community Development Advocates of Detroit), February 2009. For the complete report, see http://datadrivendetroit.org/wp-content/uploads/2010/09/CDAD_Revitalization_Framework_2010.pdf

14   Ibid.

15   Ibid.

16   Ibid.

17   Ibid.

18   For more on this project, see Karen M'Closkey and Keith VanDerSys, "Mies van der Rohe Plaza," *Magazine LW: Landscape World* 33 (June 2010), 76–85.

19   For more on the mission of this organization, see http://greeningofdetroit.com.

20   Ibid.

21   Ibid.

22   For more on the Near Westside Neighborhood Plan, see my essay "Foregrounding," in *Landscape Infrastructure: Case Studies by SWA* (Basel: Birkhäuser, 2010), 20–23.

23   Detroit hosted Formula One racing between 1982 and 1991. Racing will return to the streets of Detroit in June 2012 with the Chevrolet Detroit Belle Isle Grand Prix.

24   For a more nuanced understanding of political rights in the street, I turned to Don Mitchell, Distinguished Professor of Geography at Syracuse University. He explained in email correspondence, October 25, 2011:

      "If the (street) right of way is owned by the government, it will likely fall into what the Supreme Court calls a 'traditional public forum.' When the public forum doctrine was invented (1939) the Court more or less argued that people had an a priori right to the streets and sidewalks and parks for 'communicating issues'—but also said it could be regulated 'in the interest of all'—and for some pretty shocking reasons (such as to promote the flow of traffic or to promote 'general comfort' and 'good order'). As long as regulation was 'content neutral,' then it was likely okay. Out of this arose the permit systems that most cities use to regulate (and silence) protest. Many rights of way, though, actually run through private property (a lot of alleys are like this), and thus are not 'traditional public forums'—in fact they are not public forums at all, which is why cities can often get away with gating them off. And of course, private streets in suburbs (gated or not) might have various rights of way written into them—e.g. for cops, ambulances, fire trucks, or utility workers—but that does not mean the rest of us have access."

25   Such as by the Occupy Wall Street assembly in New York City and elsewhere. See Michael Scherer, "Taking It to the Streets," *Time*, October 24, 2011.

26   See Tyree Guyton, http://www.heidelberg.org/.

27   Ibid.

28   For more on the potential of land banking, see Genesee County Land Bank, http://www.thelandbank.org/.

29   Many thanks to Gary Hurand, who took the time to drive me around Flint on Labor Day in 2010.

30   John Brinckerhoff Jackson, "The Word Itself," in *Discovering the Vernacular Landscape* (New Haven, Conn.: Yale University Press, 1984), 1–8.

31   John E. Douglas, Ann W. Burgess, Allen. G. Burgess, and Robert K. Ressler, *Crime Classification Manual* (Hoboken, N.J.: John Wiley & Sons, 2006), 1921.

Detroit, *Disabitato,* and the Origins of Landscape
Charles Waldheim

"Landscape in the West was itself a symptom of modern loss,
a cultural form that emerged only after humanity's primal relationship to nature had been disrupted by urbanism, commerce
and technology."
　　　—Christopher S. Wood[1]

Previous page: Gregory Crewdson,
Untitled (14), 2009, showing Rome's
abandoned Cinecittà film studios

The "Formerly Urban" conference papers and this publication raise
fundamental and timely questions for those engaged in the urban
arts and allied design disciplines concerned with the contemporary
city, inviting an inversion of the temporality implied in the ideology
of urbanization.[2] This questioning of the inevitability of growth
implied in the urban disciplines also raises questions regarding the
relations between the design professions. It brings to the fore, as well,
fundamental questions about the historical construction and current
commitments of architecture, urban design, and planning.

The origins and epistemologies of the design disciplines reveal foun-
dational ideological investments in models of growth, expansion, and
ongoing development. Architecture plays a particularly significant
role here as the ur-discipline of the urban arts, as the field's professional identity has been bound up in an ideology dependent on ongoing
growth. This professional bias in favor of architecture as the progenitor
of urbanism produces an ideological blind spot as urban decline,
decay, or demise are rendered meaningless through an inability to
conceive of them.

The French philosopher Michel de Certeau has referred to this disciplinary blind spot as a professionally constructed inability to articulate
the conditions outside the limits of one's sphere of action. In a chapter
of *The Practice of Everyday Life* titled "The Unnamable," de Certeau
describes the medical profession's inability to think beyond its osten-
sible object of study: "The dying man falls outside the thinkable, which
is identified with what one can do. In leaving the field circumscribed by
the possibilities of treatment, it enters a region of meaninglessness."[3]

This condition of professionally constructed meaninglessness is
particularly evident in the inability of architecture to offer meaningful
frameworks for describing or intervening upon the city in the context
of urban abandonment, disinvestment, and decay. Over the past
decade this inability to imagine the end of growth has fueled a range
of alternative or critical discourses in the design disciplines responsible
for the city. Among them, the contemporary discourse around so-called

shrinking cities has emerged as particularly relevant and timely.[4]
The "Formerly Urban" project promises to augment and extend that
discourse with particular relevance for a range of disciplinary formations and cultural conditions attendant to contemporary urbanism in
North America. In this context, Detroit has emerged as an international
exemplar of the decentralization, dispersal, and decay of the dying
postindustrial city.

Detroit
In the second half of the twentieth century, the city of Detroit—once
the fourth-largest city in the United States—lost over half its population. The Motor City, synonymous with the automobile industry itself,
began a process of decentralization as early as the 1920s, catalyzed by
Henry Ford's decision to relocate production outside the city. While
similar conditions can be found in virtually every industrial city in
North America, Detroit recommends itself as the clearest, most legible
example of these trends evidenced in the spatial and social conditions
of the postwar American city.

In August 1990, Detroit's City Planning Commission authored a
remarkable and virtually unprecedented report.[5] This immodest
document proposed the decommissioning and abandonment of the
most vacant areas of what had been one of the most prosperous cities
in the United States. With the publication of the *Detroit Vacant Land
Survey*, Detroit's city planners documented a process of depopulation
and disinvestment that had been under way since the 1950s. With an
incendiary 1993 press release based on the City Planning Commission's
recommendations from the 1990 report, the city ombudsman, Marie
Farrell-Donaldson, publicly called for the discontinuation of services
to, and the relocation of vestigial populations from, the most vacant
portions of the city: "The city's ombudsman…is essentially suggesting
that the most blighted bits of the city should be closed down. Residents
would be relocated from dying areas to those that still had life in them.
The empty houses would be demolished and empty areas fenced off;
they would either be landscaped, or allowed to return to 'nature.'"[6]
What was remarkable about the 1990 *Detroit Vacant Land Survey* was
its unsentimental and surprisingly clear-sighted acknowledgment of
a process of postindustrial de-densification that continues to this day
in cities produced by modern industrialization. Equally striking was
how quickly the report's recommendations were angrily dismissed in
spite of the fact that they corroborated a practice of urban erasure that
was already well under way.

Also remarkable about the *Detroit Vacant Land Survey* and the city of Detroit's plan to decommission parts of itself was not its impossibility but rather the simple fact that it dared to articulate for public consumption the idea that the city was already abandoning itself. In a graphically spare document featuring maps blacked out with marker to indicate areas of vacant land, Detroit's planners rendered an image of a previously unimaginable urbanism of erasure that was already a material fact. The possibility of publicly planned demolition programs was anticipated by cultural theorist Paul Virilio: "One last question must now be asked: during a crisis period, will the demolition of cities replace the major public works of traditional politics? If so, it would no longer be possible to distinguish between the nature of recessions (economic, industrial) and the nature of war."[7]

Over the course of the 1990s, the city of Detroit lost approximately 1 percent of its housing stock annually to arson, primarily due to Devil's Night vandalism. Publicly, the city administration decried this astonishingly direct and specific critique of the city's rapidly deteriorating social conditions. Simultaneously, the city privately corroborated the arsonists' illegal intent by developing, funding, and implementing one of the largest and most sweeping demolition programs in the history of American urbanism. This program continued throughout the '90s, largely supported by the city's real estate, business, and civic communities. This curious arrangement allowed both the disenfranchised and the propertied interests to publicly blame each other for the city's problems while providing a legal and economic framework within which to carry out an ongoing process of urban erasure. Vast portions of Detroit were erased through this combination of unsanctioned burning and subsequently legitimized demolition. The combined impact of these two activities, each deemed illicit by differing interests, was to coordinate the public display of social unrest with administration attempts to erase the visual residue of Detroit's ongoing demise.

For the architectural profession, the city of Detroit in the '90s entered a condition of meaninglessness precisely because it no longer required the techniques of growth and development that had become the modus operandi of the discipline. Absent the need for these tools, Detroit became a "non-site" for the architect in the same sense that de Certeau's dead body ceased to operate as a "site" for the physician's attention. As the city decommissioned itself, it entered a condition that could not be *thought* by the architectural and planning disciplines.

As Dan Hoffman put it, in the early '90s "unbuilding surpassed building as the city's primary architectural activity."[8]

At the end of the twentieth century, at least seventy urban centers in the United States were engaged in an ongoing process of abandonment, disinvestment, and decay. While most Americans for the first time in history now live in or in close proximity to a metropolitan center, those metro areas continue to decentralize. In spite of decade-long attempts to "revitalize" the city with the construction of theaters, sports stadiums, casinos, and other publicly subsidized, privately owned, for-profit destination entertainment, Detroit continues to steadily lose population and building stock. In spite of a massive federally funded advertising campaign and a small army of census takers, both the 2000 and 2010 censuses showed Detroit's population continuing to shrink.

Reconsidering the "formerly urban" as a unique framework for thought suggests the need to develop models, cases, theories, and practices for these sites and subjects. It also recommends the requisite disciplinary and professional realignments implied in the topic. Among these, architecture as the building block of the traditional city finds itself increasingly incapable of responding in the wake of the decreased density and friction of social interaction, the increased horizontality and dispersion of urban events, and the attenuation and deterioration of building fabric as the traditional city recedes. As building fabric, street wall, and traditional public space recede as the primary determinants of urban order, landscape emerges as among the only media capable of restoring some form of spatial or social order. For this reason, for many across a range of disciplines the medium of landscape has emerged as uniquely suited to the description of and intervention in the formerly urban. As we will see bound up in the very origins of landscape, it offers a cultural milieu and medium of design equally at ease with natural succession and cultivation, existing description, and new intervention. In this regard, landscape has emerged in recent years as offering a new disciplinary framework for approaching sites of the formerly urban.[9]

Origins

It has been long established that landscape as a cultural form emerged at the same moment in two of the most urban, densely settled, and economically developed regions in western Europe.[10] Landscape is by definition an urban cultural construct, necessarily dependent upon a complex division of labor and mature markets for cultural production and consumption. It has equally been established that landscape emerged in the West as a genre of painting and theatrical arts, well before it was adopted as a way of seeing or mode of subjectivity and long before it became concerned with physical interventions in the built or natural environment.

While there is a vigorous ongoing debate as to the first paintings to be considered landscapes, the first written reference to landscape was in a 1521 record of a Venetian collection containing several Flemish paintings.[11] As a product of highly evolved mercantile economies, landscape painting emerged in the context of the Italian Renaissance, nearly a century prior to its first usage in English, as an embodiment of ornamental work devoted to the elaborate depiction of backgrounds. In so doing, landscape paintings allowed for the representation of technical virtuosity and distinction of the artistic capability of individual painters. This development of the painted background as evidence of the painterly mastery of a particular artist formed a necessary precondition for the acquisition of status value and enhanced exchange value of the painting as a commodity.[12]

The very origins of landscape have equally been informed by and are historically bound up with the depopulation, abandonment, and decay of previously urbanized territories. Rather than a recent topic of limited scope or marginal value, landscape's engagement with urban abandonment has a long history, one that goes directly to the origins of landscape as a cultural form in the West. This rereading of the history of landscape has the potential to reposition contemporary debates on landscape as a medium of urban order, particularly in the context of ongoing urban and economic restructuring, globally.

In his canonical essay "The Word Itself," J. B. Jackson described the etymology of "landscape" in the English language. Jackson found that "a landscape is a 'portion of land which the eye can comprehend at a glance.' Actually when it was first introduced…into English it did not mean the view itself, it meant a *picture* of it."[13] The *Oxford English Dictionary* corroborates Jackson's account with an early seventeenth-century reference to landscape as a "picture representing natural inland scenery, as distinguished from a sea picture, a portrait, etc." It was over a century later, in 1725, before a second definition had emerged, in which landscape had become a "view or prospect of natural inland scenery, such as can be taken in at a glance from one point of view; a piece of country scenery."[14] In this sequence of events, landscape emerged as a genre of painting first, and only a century later came to refer to a view comparable to those found in painting. Through this account, landscape becomes a way of seeing, or mode of subjectivity informed by the production and consumption of painterly images. Only from this origin can one refer to landscape in the English language as having to do with the ground itself, as seen in a particular way, and ultimately as something to be done to that ground.

By the beginning of the sixteenth century, landscape had been established in the English language as a genre of painting imported from the continent. By the seventeenth century, landscape in English migrated from a genre of painting and stage decoration into a way of seeing the world or a mode of subjectivity associated with the tour. By the eighteenth century, landscape in English had come to refer to the land looked at in this way. And by the nineteenth century, it could be used to describe the activity of refashioning the land so as to allow it to be looked at as if it were a painting. In this way, the emergence of landscape in English was to a great extent formed by the depiction of the formerly urban.

Disabitato

In the long cultural history of the formerly urban, Rome must surely be among the most significant examples available in the West. While both Detroit and Rome lost over a million residents, Detroit lost more than 50 percent of its population over just half a century. Rome lost more than 95 percent of its population over a millennium. During this time, what had been the former capital of much of the ancient world devolved into lawless wilderness before being reordered through landscape into a formerly urban interior hinterland of cultivation and succession. The city that had been host to over a million citizens at the height of its empire slumped into several centuries of decline and decay without benefit of a census. By the time the population was recorded again in the ninth century, the city's population had collapsed to less than 5 percent of its second-century peak. At its nadir, what was left of the capital was barely a medieval village clustered along the banks of the Tiber for the available water. As Howard Hibbard described it, "In the Middle Ages and Renaissance, Rome lay like a shrunken nut within her shell of antique walls."[15]

The Bufalini map of 1551 (reprinted by G. B. Nolli in the eighteenth century) illustrates the extent to which the vast territory of Rome within the Aurelian wall circuit had been given over to a formerly urban condition conflating wilderness, ancient ruins, and agricultural lands. In hot summers, carefully cultivated vineyards alongside abandoned monuments would offer grapes; in cold winters, wolves would traverse the ramparts of the Vatican gardens in search of food. By the time of Bufalini's depiction of this territory, the term *disabitato*, which had entered the language in general usage in the fourteenth century, had come to serve as a specific place-name designating the formerly urban territory within the Aurelian Walls. The fact that the generic Italian term for abandoned urban land in the fourteenth century would predate its usage as a specific place-name for Rome in the sixteenth century suggests that there would have been many other formerly urban sites being reinhabited as part of the intellectual and political project of the Italian Renaissance, as well as its economic and cultural corollaries. Equally significant is the idea that while the abandoned formerly urban territory of Rome within the walls persisted in various states of depopulation for well over a millennium, a specific place-name (and attendant conceptual framework) for this territory was itself relatively late in coming. Ultimately disabitato came to refer to the specific territory inside the Roman walls in the sixteenth century that served as a site for the papal reconstruction of Rome's urban structure as pilgrimage destination and capital of the Catholic Church in the sixteenth century.[16]

In his classic account of Rome from Christian antiquity through the Middle Ages, *Rome: Profile of a City, 312–1308*, Richard Krautheimer described the disabitato as an enormous interior agrarian hinterland that endured as late as the 1870s when it was denuded of its verdancy in favor of the modern archeological imperative. "Beyond the populous quarters and the big mansions, the disabitato extended north, east and south to the Aurelian Walls, given over mostly to fields, vineyards, and pastures."[17] In his account, Charles L. Stinger described the experience of a traveler having traversed the Roman Campagna and entering the ancient walls: "Once safely within the walls of the Eternal City, the mid-fifteenth century traveler saw before him a cityscape not remarkably different from the countryside he had just traversed. The Aurelian Walls, built for a population in excess of one million, still defended the city, but vast stretches (the *disabitato*) were given over to gardens, vineyards, and orchards, and much simply lay overgrown and abandoned."[18]

The available visual evidence of the state of the Roman disabitato is ample and predates the development of specific landscape paintings of the territory. As early as the mid-sixteenth century, Maarten van Heemskerck's sketches provided visual evidence of the Roman disabitato, as did those of Hieronymus Cock, among others. By the end of the sixteenth century, following the political consolidation and urban reconstruction projects of the Counter-Reformation Catholic Church, no fewer than four ambitious maps of Rome had been executed (by Du Pérac-Lafrérly, Cartaro, Brambilla, and Tempesta), each depicting the extent and character of the disabitato.[19]

These various sketches, views, and maps described the Roman Forum as invaded with kitchen gardens and livestock, while the less populous periphery of the disabitato persisted as wilderness in spite of the aggressive urban sanitization campaign of the church. In between the rapidly revivifying urban core and the formerly urban wilderness beyond, a kind of suburban villa landscape was interspersed with pilgrimage sites, agricultural lands, infrastructural fragments, and ancient monuments despoiled of their stone. As John Dixon Hunt described it: "Maps of both sixteenth and seventeenth centuries showed Rome as an intricate mixture of gardens and cultivated land…Falda's 1676 map of Rome…shows gardens filling not only the bastions of the city fortifications but the open spaces between ruins of classical baths and temples. Everywhere that travelers looked in the Eternal City gardens, modern gardens, seemed part of a larger classical landscape."[20]

The particular landscape described by the term disabitato at the time of its coinage as a specific place-name might best be characterized as the juxtaposition, commingling, and ongoing competition between cultivation and succession. Cultivation of gardens, groves, and vineyards could be described by the Roman concept of *villeggiatura*, or the culture of summer retreat to an agricultural setting. A century after Pope Sixtus V's ambitious urban restructuring of the capital, Falda's *Plan of Rome* in 1676 and subsequent publication of *Li Giardini di Roma* in 1683 documented in great detail the domesticated landscape of cultivated gardens and managed agricultural landscapes that the disabitato of the Baroque era had become. An example of this would be Falda's detailed depiction of the modern improvements by the Duke of Parma to the gardens of the Orti Farnesiani on the Palatine Hill.[21] Taken together, Falda's map and plates contribute to an overall sense of the disabitato in the seventeenth century as a largely cultivated suburban realm in which modest villas and vast private gardens contribute to an increasingly domesticated agricultural realm. By the time of Nolli's *La Nuova Topografia di Roma* in 1748, vineyards, orchards, vegetable gardens, nurseries, and other agricultural uses came to occupy a large and growing majority of the parcels of land in the disabitato.[22]

In contrast to this cultivated landscape, much of the disabitato persisted well into the nineteenth century as a site of spontaneous natural succession and the dynamic interplay between aggressive exotic species and their well-adapted local counterparts. As late as 1855, the English botanist Richard Deakin was able to document 420 species of plants growing spontaneously in and around the ruins of the Colosseum. In his *Flora of the Colosseum of Rome*, Deakin described over fifty varieties of grasses and dozens of wild flowers. He accounted for the presence of several exotic species through their persistent reproductive potential borne through the digestive tracts and upon the fur of animals brought to the site to take part in gladiatorial combat.[23] For many English tourists of the eighteenth and nineteenth centuries, the juxtaposition of classical ruins with spontaneous and adaptive plant communities and cultivated gardens came to embody the classical tradition itself. For many who made the tour to Rome, and for many, many more who could not make the tour but would consume its contents through representations, the cultural construction of landscape came to be shaped by paintings of the Roman disabitato. As often as not, these paintings were made by resident French painters, who worked on site to document the juxtaposition of cultivated gardens and successional plant material set among classical ruins. The English-language formulation of the term "landscape," first articulated in 1603, would come to be disproportionately represented by a painter of Roman landscapes born to the name Claude in the Duchy of Lorraine one year later.[24]

Claude's Landscapes

Claude Lorrain's landscape paintings came to construct the visual image of classical Rome abandoned and overgrown. In a range of paintings produced in Rome between the late 1620s and early 1680s such as *Caprice with Ruins of the Roman Forum* (c. 1634), Claude came to shape the English-language construction of landscape itself in the eighteenth and nineteenth centuries. Historian Richard Rand goes further, arguing that Claude "revolutionized painting in the western tradition. During a lengthy career spent almost entirely in Rome… Claude perfected a form of landscape painting that would remain influential well into the nineteenth century."[25]

Claude was orphaned by age twelve and traveled to Italy to pursue apprenticeships as an ornamental designer and pastry chef. Following apprenticeships with artists in Naples and Rome, Claude produced his first drawings from nature between 1627 and 1628 and dates his first landscape painting, *Landscape with Cattle and Peasants,* in 1628. Both his early drawings and paintings are informed by sketching tours in the disabitato and Roman Campagna. In the early 1630s, he lived in Rome near the Piazza di Spagna as part of the immigrant artist community and was admitted to the Accademia di San Luca, the official guild of Italian painters and sculptors. By 1635 he began the practice of recording detailed drawings of each painting he executed to form his *Liber Veritatis (Book of Truth),* which he maintained as evidence of the provenance of his original paintings until his death in 1682.

By the late 1630s, Claude's patrons represented the political leadership of the day from princes to kings as well as the hierarchy of the church from cardinals to popes. As Claude's reputation grew, his paintings were sought after, acquired, and commissioned by international collectors across Europe. By the time of his death, his work was held in many of the elite collections across the continent. Over the century following his death, Claude's landscape paintings and drawings would come to be disproportionately acquired by English connoisseurs for their private collections, and many of those private holdings would eventually be bequeathed to public institutions such as the British Museum, where Claude's *Liber Veritatis* is housed today.

Among Claude's innovations in landscape painting was his practice of sketching from nature in the open air. Claude developed this technique to inform the spatial motifs for larger paintings and to provide detailed depictions of plant material and qualities of light. Often these studies from subjects in the disabitato would come to form a portion of more elaborate painting subjects completed in his studio, and the sketches that informed those paintings would come to contribute to engravings and drawings from the same subject matter.[26] From his house near Piazza di Spagna, Claude regularly made day trips to numerous sites in the Roman disabitato and the immediate Roman Campagna outside its walls. Claude made frequent use of visits to sites in the immediate vicinity of Saint Peter's, the Colosseum, Circo Massimo, Palatine Hill, and the sites of ancient ruins that were available throughout the disabitato. He would also walk along the ancient routes of the Via Appia Antica and Via Tiburtina, en route to sites in the Roman Campagna. Claude would often be in the company of other artists for these excursions, as well as an armed escort.[27]

The site of the Roman Forum of Campo Vaccino was a particular favorite of Claude's, and in the mid-1630s he produced a range of related images in service of a painting, including a drawing with brown ink and brown wash on paper, an etching of the drawing on white paper, and a sketch in red chalk with brown ink and brown wash. He was also particularly adept at using pencil, ink, and wash on-site to capture the line and texture of trees and other details—often details that would inform future larger works executed in the studio. Claude's *A Study of an Oak Tree* as well as his *Trees in the Vigna of the Villa Madama, Rome*, both c. 1638, are indicative of his work on-site.

Claude's landscape paintings of the Roman disabitato would come to provide a model for English picturesque designers, but many also emulated his drawings. Richard Payne Knight, a proponent of picturesque landscape theory, owned an impressive collection of Claude drawings that he gave to the British Museum in 1824. Claude scholar Richard Rand described the acquisition and reception of Claude's paintings and drawings by popularizers of English landscape gardening: "Of the nearly 1,200 extant drawings by Claude, some 500, including the *Liber Veritatis*…are owned by the British Museum. Such is the splendor of the collection that Thomas Cole, while visiting London in the late 1820s, spent a day at the Museum looking through them. This would have been shortly after the bequest of Richard Payne Knight, whose collection of more than 261 drawings by or attributed to Claude is particularly rich in nature studies."[28]

For many consumers of Claude landscapes, the paintings and drawings in English collections served as the inspiration for a tour of the classical sites of Rome. For these English taking the grand tour, Claude's landscapes provided the itinerary and subject matter for their trips through the disabitato and into the surrounding Campagna.

According to historian Jeremy Black, for these grand tourists "shifting and contrasting views of Britain interacted with the complex presentation of Italy that drew on the strong influence of a classical education and of a public ideology that was heavily based on Classical images and themes.…These contrasts were interpreted, even 'contexted,' not only in the debate about tourism, but also in terms of another cultural product for which eighteenth-century Britain was famous: landscape gardening."[29] For Black this Anglicization of classical motifs of retreat and beauty interpreted through the Roman led to English landscapes that directly emulated the classical sites of the tour. In this context, the new landscape design "derived in large part from artistic models, especially the presentation of the landscapes of Roman Italy in the paintings of Claude Lorraine."[30] John Dixon Hunt corroborates this account, claiming that Claude's work "would have been known to travelers long before they were copied by artists like John Wooton in the 1720s or circulated later in engravings. These landscapes from Italy were mainly idealized scenes…whether the pastoral landscapes of Claude or the wilder scenes with banditti.…This ideal art was particularly attractive to those who advocated a new style in gardening, for it provided apt visual images for the ideas of paradise and the golden age, with which gardens were associated."[31] In *The Picturesque Garden in Europe*, Hunt elaborates on the reception of Claude's seventeenth-century images for English landscape tastes in the eighteenth century. Hunt argues that with the work of William Kent "the picturesque begins to play a major and an acknowledged role in garden design.… [Kent] knew his Claude Lorrain—both from Lord Burlington's 1727 purchase of the *Liber Veritatis* and presumably from his own sighting of Claude paintings and drawings during his years in Rome."[32]

The reception of Claude's work would go on to inform the development of English picturesque landscape tastes through the eighteenth and into the nineteenth century. From William Gilpin's understanding of picturesque principles for landscape gardens, through Thomas Gray's advocacy for picturesque travel, to Uvedale Price's theory, the English picturesque landscape garden was conceived and perceived through the lens of Claude's paintings of Roman abandonment.[33]

One enduring example of the impact of Claude's images of the formerly urban in the origins and development of English landscape is found in one of the more obscure objects attendant to touring culture and landscape experience. This eighteenth-century invention took the form of a small handheld dark convex mirror. The device was intended to allow the artist (and tourist alike) to view a landscape in accordance with picturesque principles so as to allow it to more closely emulate a painting of Claude. As described by Ernst Gombrich, the device aided in the "transposition of local colour into a narrower range of tones. It consisted of a curved mirror with a toned surface that was appropriately often called the 'Claude glass.'"[34] Thomas Gainsborough's undated pencil sketch *Man Holding a Mirror* shows the intended use of the glass in the mid-eighteenth century, as a landscape tourist sits with his back to the view and peers at the landscape reflected through its darkened reflection in a mirror so as to more fully apprehend the view.

Conclusions

> "So convincing was his example and so great was his influence
> that, by the late nineteenth century, landscape would become
> arguably the dominant genre of painting in Europe and America....
> There is...an obvious relationship of mood and sensibility, if not
> theme, between Claude's serene and idyllic vision of Italian coun-
> tryside and the edenic landscape tradition of nineteenth-century
> American culture."
> —Richard Rand[35]

Claude's representations of the Roman disabitato, through the
reception of his work in discussions of English landscape gardening,
came to stand for the very image of landscape as a cultural form in
much of the West. This particular form, this image of landscape,
and all that it implies about contemporary design culture continue
to exert an enormous ambient influence on the discipline to this day.
Any attempt to engage in critical reflection on this inheritance, or to
engage in practices that elide or evade it, must first come to terms
with this history and its oft-repeated, dimly illuminated, anemic
reflections. Any attempt to argue for a renewed engagement with the
contemporary cultural status of landscape architecture must surely
begin with a close reading of its past.

The status of the formerly urban recommends a rereading of the origins
of landscape in the West. As a cultural category uniquely available to
the problematic of sites and subjects of former urbanity, landscape
might be usefully resituated as medium and method through which the
formerly urban might aspire to the social, environmental, and cultural
conditions of the urban, absent its traditional architectonic forms.

Research in support of this essay was made possible by the generous support of the Prince
Charitable Trusts Rome Prize in Landscape Architecture and Residential Fellowship at the
American Academy in Rome.

1   Christopher S. Wood, *Albrecht Altdorfer and the Origins of Landscape*
      (Chicago: University of Chicago Press, 1993), 25.

2   The "Formerly Urban: Projecting Rust Belt Futures" conference was held at Syracuse
      University School of Architecture in Syracuse, N.Y., on October 13–14, 2010.

3   Michel de Certeau, *The Practice of Everyday Life*, trans. Steven Rendall
      (Berkeley: University of California Press, 1984), 190.

4   While the topic of shrinkage was manifest in the work of several American academics and
      theorists dealing with urban restructuring through the 1990s, the German Federal Cultural
      Foundation gave it greater visibility in 2002 with the funding of a multiyear research
      program under the English-language title "Shrinking Cities" and led by Philipp Oswalt.
      See Shrinking Cities, http://www.shrinkingcities.com/. For information on their program of
      events, exhibitions, working papers, and publications, see also Philipp Oswalt and others,
      eds., *Shrinking Cities*, vols. 1 and 2 (Berlin: Hatje Cantz, 2006); and Philipp Oswalt, ed., *Atlas
      of Shrinking Cities* (Berlin: Hatje Cantz, 2006).

5   City of Detroit City Planning Commission, *Detroit Vacant Land Survey*, August 24, 1990.

6   "Day of the Bulldozer," *The Economist*, May 8, 1993, 33–34.

7   See Paul Virilio, "The Overexposed City," in *Zone 1/2*, ed. Michel Feher and Sanford Kwinter,
      trans. Astrid Hustvedt (New York: Zone Books, 1987). In 1998, Detroit's mayor, Dennis Archer,
      secured $60 million in loan guarantees from the U.S. Department of Housing and Urban
      Development to finance the demolition of every abandoned residential building in the city.
      See also Alyssa Katz, "Dismantling the Motor City," *Metropolis*, June 1998, 33.

8   Dan Hoffman, "Erasing Detroit," in *Stalking Detroit*, ed. Georgia Daskalakis,
      Charles Waldheim, and Jason Young (Barcelona: Actar, 2001), 100–103.

9   For more on the recent discourse on landscape urbanism, see Charles Waldheim,
      "Motor City," in *Shaping the City: History, Theory, and Urban Design*, ed. Rodolphe
      El-Khoury and Edward Robbins (London: Routledge, 2003), 79–99; and Charles Waldheim,
      "Introduction" and "Landscape as Urbanism," in *The Landscape Urbanism Reader*
      (New York: Princeton Architectural Press, 2006), 13–19, 35–53.

10   Cultural geographer Denis Cosgrove argues that landscape "first emerged as a recognized
      genre in the most economically advanced, densest settled and most highly urbanized
      regions of fifteenth-century Europe: in Flanders and upper Italy." See Denis Cosgrove, *Social
      Formation and Symbolic Landscape* (Madison: University of Wisconsin Press, 1984), 20.

11   E. H. Gombrich, "The Renaissance Theory of Art and the Rise of Landscape," in *Gombrich
      on the Renaissance—Volume 1: Norm and Form* (New York and London: Phaidon Press,
      1985), 107–21.

12   Cosgrove, *Social Formation and Symbolic Landscape*, 87–88.

13   J. B. Jackson, "The Word Itself," in *Discovering the Vernacular Landscape* (New Haven,
      Conn.: Yale University Press, 1984), 1–8.

14   "Landscape," *Oxford English Dictionary*, 2nd ed. (Oxford: Oxford University Press, 1989),
      628–29.

15   See Howard Hibbard, *Carlo Maderno and Roman Architecture 1580–1630* (London:
      Zwemmer, 1971). For further characterization of Rome's recession in late antiquity, see also
      Bertrand Lançon, *Rome in Late Antiquity: Everyday Life and Urban Change AD 312–609*,
      trans. Antonia Nevill (Edinburgh: Edinburgh University Press, 2000).

16   The *Dizionario Etimologico Italiano* (p. 1321) describes *disabitato* as a transitive reflexive form of "abitare," the verb for dwell or inhabit. On the sequence and timing of *disabitato* as a generic term and a specific place-name, see Richard Krautheimer, *Rome: Profile of a City, 312–1308* (Princeton, NJ: Princeton University Press, 1980); and Gerhart B. Ladner's book review of Krautheimer's *Rome: Profile of a City, 312–1308,* in *The Art Bulletin* 65, no. 2 (June 1983): 336–39.

17   Krautheimer, *Rome,* 256.

18   Charles L. Stinger, *The Renaissance in Rome* (Bloomington: Indiana University Press, 1985).

19   Maarten van Heemskerck, *Sketchbook,* 1534–36; Hieronymus Cock, *Sketchbook,* 1558; Du Pérac-Lafrérly, *View of Rome,* 1575; Du Pérac-Lafrérly, *Map of Rome,* 1577; Cartaro, *Map of Rome,* 1576; Brambilla, *Map of Rome,* 1590; and Tempesta, *Map of Rome,* 1593.

20   John Dixon Hunt, *Garden and Grove: The Italian Renaissance Garden in the English Imagination, 1600–1750* (Philadelphia: University of Pennsylvania Press, 1996), 21, 32.

21   G. B. Falda, *Map of Rome,* 1676; and G. B. Falda, *Li Giardini di Roma,* 1683.

22   G. B. Nolli, *La Nuova Topografia di Roma,* 1748. See also James Tice, "The Forgotten Landscape of Rome: the *Disabitato,*" April 15, 2005, http://nolli.uoregon.edu/disabitato.html. Accessed June 15, 2007.

23   Richard Deakin, *Flora of the Colosseum of Rome; or, Illustrations and Descriptions of Four Hundred and Twenty Plants Growing Spontaneously Upon the Ruins of the Colosseum of Rome* (London: Groombridge and Sons, 1855). For further context on Deakin's depiction of spontaneous vegetation among the ruins, see Christopher Woodward, *In Ruins* (London: Vintage, 2001), 23–24.

24   Cosgrove, *Social Formation and Symbolic Landscape,* 158.

25   Richard Rand, *Claude Lorrain—The Painter as Draftsman: Drawings from the British Museum* (New Haven, Conn.: Yale University Press, 2006); Michael Kitson, *Claude Lorrain, Liber Veritatis* (London: British Museum, 1978); Marcel Roethlisberger, *Claude Lorrain: The Paintings,* vols. 1 and 2 (New Haven, Conn.: Yale University Press, 1961); and Marcel Roethlisberger, *Claude Lorrain: The Drawings,* vols. 1 and 2 (Berkeley: University of California Press, 1968).

26   Rand, *Claude Lorrain,* 52–53.

27   Ibid., 58.

28   Ibid., 23.

29   Jeremy Black, *Italy and the Grand Tour* (New Haven, Conn.: Yale University Press, 2003), 205.

30   Black, *Italy and the Grand Tour,* 205.

31   John Dixon Hunt, *The Figure in the Landscape: Poetry, Painting, and Gardening during the Eighteenth Century* (Baltimore, Md.: Johns Hopkins University Press, 1989), 39–43.

32   John Dixon Hunt, *The Picturesque Garden in Europe* (London: Thames and Hudson, 2002), 34.

33   For example, see William Gilpin's *Remarks on Forest Scenery* (1791) as referenced in Dixon
      Hunt, *The Picturesque Garden in Europe*, 337–38; and Uvedale Price's *An Essay on the
      Picturesque* (1794) as referenced in Dixon Hunt, *The Picturesque Garden in Europe*, 351.

34   E. H. Gombrich, "From Light into Paint," and "The Image in the Clouds," in *Art and Illusion:
      A Study in the Psychology of Pictorial Representation*, 6th ed. (New York and London:
      Phaidon Press, 2002), 29–54, 154–69.

35   Rand, *Claude Lorrain*, 22.

Underwriting Icicles and Leveraging Sidewalks

Marc Norman

Throughout the Sun Belt—and particularly in "sand states" like Florida, Arizona, Nevada, and California—thousands of empty suburban houses languish on the market. Suburban and exurban shopping centers and malls deteriorate for lack of tenants. Financed as speculative real estate investments during the boom years of the early 2000s, they either never found buyers or were emptied by bank foreclosures as capital evaporated during the financial crisis that started in 2007.

Previous page: Fig. 1. Icicles serve as a manifestation of energy inefficiency

Many of these investments were financed with mortgage-backed securities and other financial products created to capture a portion of the world's investment capital. This "Giant Pool of Money," as outlined in Adam Davidson's award-winning NPR exposé on the collapse of the housing market, represents the accumulated funds of insurance companies, pension funds, central banks, and other institutional investors seeking returns in global markets. The available capital in Davidson's estimation is $70 trillion.[1]

While these funds created the explosive growth of homes and businesses in the Sun Belt and other booming exurban locations, Rust Belt cities suffered continued disinvestment. In the present financial crisis, with former boom towns overbuilt and mortgage lending tight, the investment funds are seeking alternative outlets. How can we redirect this capital to Rust Belt cities, where it can finance sustainable projects and promote community development?

Just as savvy financiers created mortgage-backed securities and other products to channel investment capital into Sun Belt subdivisions and isolated shopping centers, we can create financial instruments to direct investment toward revitalizing Rust Belt cities and reinforcing the social values associated with dense, transit-rich, urban communities. What we need are models that use the language of lenders and investors to evidence the value embedded in communities. By demonstrating the capacity of new kinds of investment to yield sustainable returns, these models would prove that Rust Belt cities are places of worth and stable areas for investment.

Socially motivated lending institutions, foundations, and policy organizations are already engaged in efforts to bring capital and expertise to neglected neighborhoods. Using examples from among these emerging practices, I will show how, even in the absence of the property appreciation that motivates much real estate investment, Rust Belt cities can identify inefficiencies in our existing buildings and infrastructure and craft solutions to address this waste, creating value to draw new capital to revitalize dilapidated neighborhoods. The solutions I have in mind are at once physical and social. They range from energy retrofits that capture the capital leaking out of older houses in the form of wasted heat, to planning models that recognize the value lost in car-centered suburban and exurban development patterns. In conjunction with the critical thinking on creating efficiencies, innovative financial instruments that create channels for directing investment capital toward Rust Belt revitalization also have to be developed.

Let's start by looking at real estate financing in formerly urban communities. The issues facing Rust Belt cities are manifold, but the main issue is that the funds available in the form of loans and equity (sources) do not equal or exceed the costs (uses) that are needed to maintain the good functioning of homes, businesses, and neighborhoods. Balancing these two opposing metrics, sources and uses, is the basis of real estate finance. This state of imbalance creates a collapsing house of cards for struggling communities. While social policy, design, and public resources are crucial in formulating a solution for Rust Belt communities, this fundamental, structural impediment cannot be ignored. Innovative financing models can provide the solution.

Neighborhoods faced with declining populations, a diminishing jobs base, and aging housing stock create a cycle of disinvestment. Traditional lenders and investors look at low-wealth communities and see only risk, so they steer their money elsewhere. The result in such neighborhoods: building maintenance is suspended, requests for loans are declined, and houses are increasingly abandoned. It is hard to break this cycle once it begins.

In the absence of increasing values, Rust Belt cities have traditionally relied on subsidies to arrest decline and to stabilize neighborhoods. Under this strategy, cities look to philanthropy as well as to federal, state, and local sources for money to cover the gaps between sources and uses. Subsidy programs are important in revitalizing low-wealth communities, since they often go in where private investment capital will not. This is accomplished through loans at below-market interest rates, grants to reduce the amounts that need to be financed, or "first-loss" funding that lowers the risk for other investors. But subsidies cannot be the sole solution, as they are subject to the whims of shifting electoral results, competing policy objectives, and budgeting priorities. The subsidy model is not sustainable, particularly now that many

formerly stable markets are falling into long-term decline and clam-
oring for their share of philanthropic or governmental largess. Subsidies
also tend to be skewed toward particular priorities not necessarily
aligned with the creation of healthy communities. In the case of Rust
Belt cities, federal dollars have historically supported home ownership
over renters' needs, and have funded mega-projects, like stadiums and
shopping malls, at the expense of small independent businesses.

To complement subsidy programs and increase the total volume of
investment in Rust Belt cities, we need to adapt traditional financing
mechanisms so that they provide more sustainable solutions that
address systems rather than particular aspects within the system.
If private investors see value in our cities, they will provide the sources
currently missing and create an environment where a more sustainable
model works. Fortunately, this approach has gained significant traction
over the last decade. The process started with foundations, socially
motivated investors, and community developers, and has recently
engaged traditional financial advisors and large corporations.
These funders are engaged in the emerging field of triple bottom
line investing: a financial return first and foremost, but also a social
return in the sense that the lives of citizens are made better, and
an environmental return in reduced dependence on fossil fuels. In the
"Giant Pool of Money" mentioned earlier, Davidson says, "A global
army of investment managers was hungrier and twitchier than ever
before. They all wanted the same thing: a nice low-risk investment
that paid some return." They believed wrongly that mortgage-backed
securities were this "low-risk investment." They were not. With the
collapse of traditional investment vehicles, interest in triple bottom
line investing has grown substantially.[2]

Fig. 2. Loan-to-value chart

Typical Property	Amount	Categories	Loan Calculation
Assumed Value	$100,000	Rental Income (monthly)	$1200
Loan to Value (LTV)	80%	Expenses	$800
Maximum Loan	$80,000	Debt Service Coverage (DSC)	1.25
		Available for Loan Payment	(400 ÷ 1.25 = 320)
		Interest Rate	6.00%
		Term of Loan	15 years
		Maximum Loan	$35,550

The adoption of traditional financing methods to support community development in formerly urban communities is poised to expand beyond this circle of initial players. But bringing more capital to this field will require that communities learn the concepts and language of finance while investors learn to assess the needs and potentials of Rust Belt communities. In formulating solutions that rely less on public subsidies, or on continual property appreciation, Rust Belt cities can become a laboratory for ways that communities find a path back to stability. The innovations developed in formerly urban locations such as these can then spread to a broader range of contexts, supporting positive outcomes in an expanded field of locations.

Defining Sources and Uses

Capital flows into or out of communities depending on lenders' willingness to invest in them in expectation of a financial return. Rust Belt cities have a number of structural problems—such as diminishing populations, low real estate prices, and lack of employment opportunities—that make them less attractive to lenders and investors.

Traditional underwriting standards work against shrinking cities, because loans are based on cash flow or a percentage of value. In stable and growing markets, lending is based on expecting a year-over-year increase in rents or sales prices. But if the cost to replace or even to renovate a building exceeds its current value, private lenders will not provide capital. Under these conditions stabilizing existing buildings is crucial, but in many cases the worth of an existing building fails to meet the standards banks use to underwrite the cost of needed improvements.

Loans are typically underwritten under one of two criteria: loan-to-value (LTV) ratio or debt service coverage (DSC) ratio. For LTV, a lender will set value to a property based on comparable properties in its geographic area. He or she will then structure a loan to cover 70 to 90 percent of this value, which mitigates risk and ensures that the property owner retains a financial stake in the property. In the case of a default the lender can recoup the investment through a sale, even taking into account diminished value. With DSC the lender looks at a buyer's income, or income generated from the property, and underwrites a loan, assuming that sufficient cash flow will come from the property to pay the loan while also providing a cushion to cover any changes in conditions. The final loan will be the result of the lesser of the LTV and DSC equations (fig. 2).

Case-Shiller Price Cumulative Declines from Peak (SA), Year and City

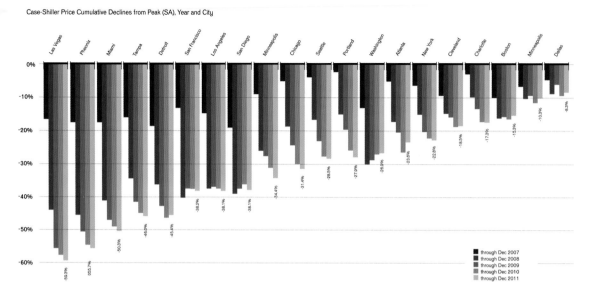

Fig. 3. Case-Shiller home price declines by region

These equations are simple, but they have complicated real-world effects. Change any part of the equation and you affect whether a neighborhood will be stable or will decline. In declining markets, refinancing becomes impossible. If homeowners' expenses increase without corresponding increases in their income, home equity financing and rehabilitation loans become impossible. If rental income declines, owners may have to choose between paying the mortgage and making needed repairs. Due to the role of comparables in LTV assessments, declining value and disinvestment are not specific to a single home or building. Like a contagion, the declining worth of one home or one block drags down the sales price on others.

This is the story of Rust Belt cities and many other communities that find themselves in a similar situation since the asset bubble popped in 2008. From their peak in 2007, U.S. home prices have declined between 7.7 percent and 53 percent, depending on location (fig. 3).[3] The result is that, as of May 2011, over 11 million homes, or 23 percent of all mortgaged homes, in this country are "underwater"—their outstanding debt exceeds their current worth.[4] Without the benefit of rising values or rising rents, the cycle of disrepair and disinvestment pulls cities and neighborhoods into a downward spiral (fig. 4). How can we bring investment back into cities experiencing this decline? Given the real

estate fundamentals of balancing sources and uses, how can finance play a role in reinvestment?

Fig. 4. Dilapidated and stable properties in Detroit, Michigan

Underwriting Icicles

An emerging area of finance that gives value to energy efficiency holds great promise in channeling capital to neglected cities and neighborhoods. Especially in the Midwest and Northeast, heating and cooling costs represent a significant portion of a building's operating expenses, so a concerted effort to reduce these costs will create additional cash flow, which can be deployed to other expenses. This method flips the

Hypothetical Family of 4	Pre-Retrofit	Post-Retrofit	Loan Terms
Building Income	$3,400 (850 x 4)	No change	
Total Expenses	$2,530 (monthly)	$2,221	$309 in savings
Management	1,200	No change	5.5% interest
Electricity/Gas	750	525	1.25 DSC
Water/Sewer	280	196	15 years
Taxes/Other	300	No change	$28,363 potential loan

Fig. 5. Energy-savings table and calculation of retrofit loans

traditional financial-underwriting equation to look at savings that can be generated from existing assets, rather than appreciation in rents or building values. Savings from energy improvements provide the assurance for repayment of retrofit loans, often at no additional cost to owners.

Studies conducted in low-income neighborhoods show that energy costs can consume from 17 to 25 percent of building occupants' income.[5] As energy costs are some of the most volatile operating expenses, lowering and controlling these costs can have a significant impact, both financially and physically, on the health of the community. For Rust Belt cities, the notion of fleshing out savings and underwriting assets based on creating efficiencies holds a great deal of promise in arresting the cycle of decline while creating a stable vehicle for investors.

Consider icicles. Formed by water that has been melted and then refrozen, they represent energy expended to negative benefit (fig. 1). Energy, of course, translates directly into dollars. While icicles evidence heating costs and the waste that comes from things like poor insulation, unrepaired roofs, or leaky windows, they also index the larger issue of investment flowing out of neighborhoods. The icicle is useful in representing not only our waste but also the possibility of capturing and underwriting value to harness savings that can be allocated to revitalization.[6]

Take a typical home for a family of four in a city such as Syracuse, New York, or Cleveland, Ohio. A lender seeking to underwrite an energy retrofit could lend an owner the funds necessary to purchase and install new insulation and other equipment. Since the loan amount would be based on the anticipated energy cost savings generated by these improvements, it would be independent from the value of the property, and the loan payments would not strain the owner's finances.

The chart in figure 5 assumes savings of 30 percent annually from various energy improvements. Even with a DSC ratio of 1.25—which assures that savings from the improvements could still provide repayment even if only a 5 percent savings is achieved to cushion against potential energy cost increases and to mitigate lender risk—a loan of over $28,000 is feasible to fund weatherization, new windows, new boilers, and other equipment. The manifold benefits include amelioration of the property, better curb appeal, lower maintenance and energy costs, and an enhanced quality of life. As the savings from the retrofit are proven out, loans of this type can build momentum for additional retrofit loans. If a significant number of properties evidence such improvements, they can serve as comparables for other properties in the area and so increase the value of those properties. If scaled up, this approach can thus improve entire neighborhoods. Demonstrated success creates investor confidence, which could potentially make loans of this type as ubiquitous and efficient as the five-year auto loan or thirty-year fixed-rate mortgage. It should be noted that these financial products, which we now take for granted, took the concerted effort of government, financial institutions, and a host of industries to become accepted and widely available.

The energy retrofit model discussed above seems to offer a simple solution to the intractable problem of deploying capital to stabilize neighborhoods. The reality is more complicated, of course, and involves cooperation among many different professions and areas of government. The model for valuing energy savings needs to be proven, with multiple parties taking the initial risk to bring these innovations into the mainstream. Even if the model is shown to be effective from a lender's perspective, it is necessary that all of the other players in real estate foster a change in thinking. Real estate investors, market analysts, appraisers, developers, mortgage insurance providers (like the State of New York Mortgage Agency), and secondary market purchasers (like Fannie Mae and Freddie Mac) will all need to get on board. With these and other government-sponsored enterprises (GSEs) responsible for over 70 percent of all mortgage activity in the United States, no program can be effective without them.[7]

While progress so far has been slow, taking shape mostly as ad hoc efforts in limited geographies, many people are coming around to this thinking, including foundations and socially motivated investors. For instance, Enterprise Community Partners, a nonprofit organization that assists in developing affordable housing, has produced "Green Community Standards" in order to systematize practices in the area of retrofits and energy efficiency. These standards, which have been accepted in the affordable housing community and adopted by a number of state and local agencies, are a start to establishing precedents for lending against projected savings.[8]

In order to foster change and expand the field of energy finance, Enterprise and similar organizations have provided guarantees, low-interest loans, technical expertise, and financing in a first-loss position

Fig. 6. A sidewalk ends.

in the event loans cannot be repaid. Governmental initiatives, such as Property Assessed Clean Energy (PACE), also help financing. A PACE bond or lien is a debt instrument whose proceeds are lent to commercial and residential property owners to finance energy retrofits that encompass efficiency measures and small renewable energy systems. Borrowers repay the loans over fifteen to twenty years via an annual assessment on their property tax bill. PACE bonds can be issued by municipal financing districts or finance companies, and the proceeds can be used to retrofit both commercial and residential properties.[9]

Other energy finance programs include the U.S. Department of Energy's $5 billion weatherization program, funded as part of the American Recovery and Reinvestment Act, which recognizes that reducing energy costs provides a host of benefits to communities. In New York State, the New York State Energy Research and Development Authority provides energy audits and grant financing to homeowners and landlords to jump-start the retrofit process.

These programs are making a difference. But to effect systematic change capable of transforming struggling communities, conventional financial institutions will have to incorporate energy savings into the way they underwrite and lend. Success in this arena could mean that even on a block with dilapidated housing, a stable homeowner could secure capital to make repairs to his or her home. It could also mean that a dilapidated home might be salvageable because a buyer would have the ability to finance improvements. In other words, using the funds generated from energy savings leverages funds available for improvements. As improvements raise the values of properties, the downward spiral we currently see could reverse and create steadily improving neighborhoods.

To this end, Living Cities—a group of foundations and institutions that fund low-income people and cities—has partnered with the Deutsche Bank Americas Foundation to commission an energy efficiency data report bringing together the fields of building science and finance to look at the effectiveness of different energy-modeling methods. By developing better predictions of how retrofits affect energy use, studying the long-term efficacy of retrofits, and building a public database, the project aims to encourage increased energy-based lending.[10]
The project has created a shared online database to support ongoing valuation of the economic and fiscal impacts of multifamily retrofits. This will allow users to identify best practices for minimizing project risk and to develop new underwriting guidelines. Currently, retrofit loans take a significant amount of governmental intervention and subsidy; if the models are proven out, such loans could become a conventional product, widely available and serving as another tool for revitalizing our struggling Rust Belt communities.

Leveraging Sidewalks
Another area where financial innovation can have an impact is smart growth. Much like energy retrofits, smart growth is a way of identifying inefficiency and putting a value on savings made by connecting improvements to quantifiable metrics (fig. 6).

While cities shrink, paradoxically their utilization of land increases. During the expansionist era of the 1950s and 1960s, many American cities were ripped apart by highway construction and suburbanization, and it is still the case that significant federal expenditures go to new highways far from city centers. This inefficiency means that increasing amounts of infrastructure are built for fewer people who are more widely dispersed.[11] As the United States develops on the

periphery, paving over farmland, it neglects the infrastructure in its cities, which further reinforces outmigration.

All too often, the subsidy model currently employed in struggling cities creates islands of development that neither connect nor benefit existing communities. With the long-term decline of cities and the rise of suburbs, it has become an assumption in many city governments that prosperity will arrive if they incorporate suburban elements into planning and development. In the hope of capturing revenue, governments subsidize suburban-like big-ticket projects—such as malls, highway bypasses, sports stadiums, and parking lots—through tax abatements, bond issuances, or direct payments.[12] Even in the face of many studies proving that the promised benefits typically do not materialize, the model of large, subsidized, single-use development marches on.[13]

Looking at maps of many cities, we can see highways and isolated shopping malls as manifestations of misdirected energy, flowing out of our cities rather than concentrated efficiently within them. Like the icicles on a building, they are physical symbols of waste and also easily identifiable locations where intervention can provide potentially profitable savings through improvements in efficiency. The concept of smart growth is simple: concentrate growth in compact configurations that are transit-oriented, walkable, and bicycle-friendly, and support development that values long-range, regional considerations of sustainability over a short-term focus. Its goals are to achieve a unique sense of community and place through adjacent and mixed-use development

Opposite, top: Fig. 7. Aerial photo of land uses, Syracuse, New York

Opposite, bottom: Fig. 8. Aerial photo of potential linkages, Syracuse, New York

Above: Fig. 9. Roberto Clemente Bridge, Pittsburgh, Pennsylvania

Annual Household Gasoline Expenses ($) 2008 Gas Prices

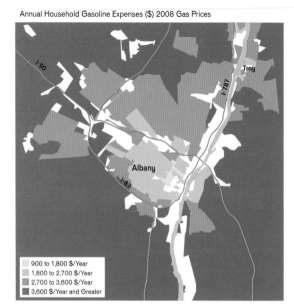

Legend:
- 900 to 1,800 $/Year
- 1,800 to 2,700 $/Year
- 2,700 to 3,600 $/Year
- 3,600 $/Year and Greater

Housing + Transportation Costs % Income

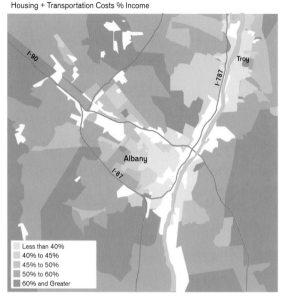

Legend:
- Less than 40%
- 40% to 45%
- 45% to 50%
- 50% to 60%
- 60% and Greater

Fig. 10. Annual household gasoline expenses (2008 gas prices) and housing and transportation costs as percent of income

and a range of housing choices. The difficulty is underwriting these concepts and showing that incorporating them into communities increases value and can generate a financial return.

As with energy retrofits, we have not established financing mechanisms to support smart growth. Lenders and investors typically default to conventional underwriting geared toward isolated developments surrounded by parking lots and new single-family subdivisions. In fact, these conditions are often mandated by the very agencies—such as the Federal Housing Finance Agency and Fannie Mae, as well as the U.S. Department of Transportation and local agencies—that are charged with supporting the financing of developments.[14]

If we develop models that show the benefits of concentrating uses and making connections, smart growth can be another area where we capture savings by finding new ways of underwriting so that capital returns to our cities. Linking jobs to housing and housing to retail can redirect income away from cars and gas, which are increasingly imported from abroad, toward wealth-producing endeavors and local commerce. If we connect and leverage existing assets in our cities, we can bring investment back. In some cases the pieces necessary for smart growth are in place, but the planning or forethought to create beneficial linkages are not (figs. 7, 8).

The question of smart-growth financing is how to quantify and understand the fiscal benefits of weaving jobs, transportation, entertainment, housing, fresh food, business centers, and recreation together. As with energy retrofits, foundations, governmental agencies, and financial institutions can instigate the development of those models. Architecture can provide coherent thinking about how to make connections to enliven and activate the public realm. If quantifying the economic and social benefits of reconnecting our communities is proven out, those benefits can be underwritten to spur investment. If we assume that investments tying into existing infrastructure and knitting adjacent uses increase value, we should be able to show that these investments can provide a financial return.

Large and small initiatives across the United States are currently doing just that. These initiatives include integrated city planning efforts such as the revitalization of Beacon, New York, which with the help of the nonprofit organization Scenic Hudson lured the Dia Art Foundation to establish an outpost in a former Nabisco factory. This effort connected the town to its waterfront and created clear linkages to existing rail infrastructure. Using long-term planning and a commitment to smart growth in transforming the city and drawing new capital, this holistic effort—incorporated with aid to local businesses and a housing plan—has led to a revitalized town in an otherwise depressed region. For contrast, one only has to peer across the river to dilapidated, crime-ridden Newburgh, New York.

On a more modest scale, the city of Pittsburgh reinvigorated a formerly derelict district through the simple act of closing Roberto Clemente Bridge to car traffic on game days for the Pirates and Steelers (fig. 9). This link between downtown and PNC Park baseball stadium created a festival atmosphere on game days and boosted pedestrian traffic and commerce in neighborhoods on both sides of the bridge. For most sports teams, fans drive in and drive out. One well thought-out modification made fans linger and redirect their capital to local businesses, contributing to the surrounding communities. In financial terms, the return on investment for the City of Pittsburgh from moving two barricades and stationing a few police officers could go head-to-head with the most complex mortgage securities during the height of the housing boom, but at present this is not how we measure success in our cities, or set priorities. As with energy retrofits, there are many one-off, neighborhood-specific examples that have shown the economic value of connection. But it will take a concerted effort on the part of many entities to test and evaluate the model on a large scale.

In New York State, the Smart Growth Public Infrastructure Policy Act of 2010 is an attempt by government to jump-start the process "for the long-term fiscal economic and environmental sustainability of the state." The act instructs state agencies, authorities, and public corporations to align their spending on infrastructure with stated smart growth criteria. It also mandates that more of New York's tax money be spent on infrastructure in compact communities and less of it in sprawling locations. By focusing infrastructure spending in developed areas, the act will protect environmental resources, foster compact, mixed-use development, and reduce dependence on automobiles.[15]

The Center for Neighborhood Technology—a Chicago-based nonprofit organization focused on sustainable development—is also helping to further this area of research by demonstrating the benefits of connection. Their work shows the substantial costs that come with a car-dependent lifestyle. While in some communities up to 28 percent of household income is spent on transportation costs, compact neighborhoods typically have commuting costs below 15 percent (fig. 10).

Another example comes from the National Neighborhood Indicators Partnership, a community-building organization of the Urban Institute and local partners. One result of the collaboration is Data Driven Detroit. Launched in 2009, this project uses geographic information systems and data sharing from many sources to evidence that focusing programs, grants, and research within the Detroit city limits will foster economic prosperity.[16]

In addition to these not-for-profit projects, profit-driven but socially motivated organizations are beginning to invest in smart growth. One example is the Rose Smart Growth Investment Fund, the first real estate fund in the United States to focus exclusively on acquiring and greening existing buildings. The premise of the fund is that existing structures are inherently greener than new construction, and locations that reduce the need for auto-based transportation are a better investment in the long term. Accordingly, it acquires real estate near transit or in walkable communities, then enhances these assets with green management practices, professional real estate skills, and a long-term investment strategy. The activities of the fund are advancing the notion that smart, environmentally conscious real estate investment strategies will yield better long-term value to both investors and low-income communities. To date it is proving out its model by improving communities while yielding double-digit returns.

Innovative thinking such as that outlined above has the capacity to stabilize our cities and even allow them to thrive. For the solutions to problems of disinvestment to be scalable and replicable, we must develop models that rely less on subsidies and that instead engage private-sector players and market motivations. Energy retrofits and smart growth are two examples of how finance can be used to address these problems and use leverage to bring capital to struggling cities. But there are many more models being formulated and tested in Rust Belt communities, including initiatives for fresh food, business incubators, and educational facilities.

Despite the current state of the world economy and ongoing disinvestment in our cities, the "Giant Pool of Money" mentioned by Davidson, which represents insurance companies, in his words, "saving for a catastrophe, pension funds saving money for retirement, the central bank of England saving for whatever central banks save for," is growing and looking for new outlets. Nascent and established initiatives like those reviewed here could provide hope for long-neglected communities. With the right data sets and financial models, we can tap into investment dollars with innovative financial projects to focus loan products and engage the capital markets to harness that capital for the revitalization of our communities.

1   See Alex Blumberg and Adam Davidson, "The Giant Pool of Money," *This American Life*,
       Chicago Public Media, May 9, 2008, http://www.thisamericanlife.org/radio-archives
       /episode/355/the-giant-pool-of-money. See also Alex Blumberg and Adam Davidson,
       "Return to the Giant Pool of Money," *This American Life*, Chicago Public Media, September
       25, 2009, http://www.thisamericanlife.org/radio-archives/episode/390/return-to-the-giant-
       pool-of-money; and Stephen Neary, Connie Li Chan, and Robin Arnott, *Planet Money's
       Toxic Asset* (video), NPR, http://www.npr.org/series/124587240/planet-money-s-toxic-asset.

2   Steven Godeke, "Philanthropy's New Passing Gear: Mission Related Investing,"
       Rockefeller Philanthropy Advisors, 2008.

3   Bill McBride, "Case Shiller: National Home Prices Hit New Low in 2011 Q1," Calculated Risk
       Blog, May 31, 2011, http://www.calculatedriskblog.com/2011/05/case-shiller-national-home-
       prices-hit.html.

4   Derek Kravitz, "Number of Underwater Mortgages Rises as More Homeowners Fall Behind,"
       Huffington Post, March 8, 2011, http://www.huffingtonpost.com/2011/03/08/number-of-
       underwater-mort_n_833000.html.

5   Enterprise Community Partners, "Building a Greener Future for America's Families,"
       July 2008, http://www.greencommunitiesonline.org/pdfs/green_fact_sheet.pdf.

6   United States Environmental Protection Agency, "Self-Sealing Bituminous Membrane in
       Cold Climates," November 2, 2010, http://www.epa.gov/indoorairplus/technical
       /moisture/1_10.html.

7   Dwight M. Jaffe, "Reforming the U.S. Mortgage Market Through Private Market Incentives,"
       George Mason University, March 2011.

8   Enterprise Green Communities, "About Green Communities," 2011,
       http://www.greencommunitiesonline.org/about.

9   North Carolina Solar Center, North Carolina State University, and the Interstate Renewable
       Energy Council, "Local Option: Municipal Sustainable Energy Programs," September 2010,
       http://www.dsireusa.org/incentives/incentive.cfm?Incentive_Code=NY68F&re=1&ee=1.

10   Julie Satow, "Showing the Benefits of 'Green' Retrofits," *New York Times*,
       New York edition, June 1, 2010, http://www.nytimes.com/2010/06/02/realestate/
       commercial/02deutsche.html.

11   Ivonne Audirac, "Urban Shrinkage Amid Fast Metropolitan Growth (Two Faces of
       Contemporary Urbanism)," in *The Future of Shrinking Cities: Problems, Patterns and
       Strategies of Urban Transformation in a Global Context*, ed. Karina Pallagst et al. (Berkeley,
       Calif.: Center for Global Metropolitan Studies, Institute of Urban and Regional Development,
       and the Shrinking Cities International Research Network, 2009).

12   Joanna Cagan and Neil De Mause, *Field of Schemes: How the Great Stadium Swindle Turns
       Public Money into Private Profit* (Lincoln, Neb.: Bison Books: 2008).

13   Sarah Wilhelm, "Public Funding of Sports Stadiums, Policy Brief," Center for Public Policy
       and Administration, University of Utah, April 2008, www.cppa.utah.edu/publications
       /finance_tax/Sports_Stadiums.pdf.

14   Marc A. Weiss, *The Rise of the Community Builders: The American Real Estate Industry and
       Urban Land Planning* (Washington, D.C.: Beard Books, 2002).

15   Sandy Stewart, "Senator Montgomery's 'Smart Growth Public Infrastructure Policy Act'
      Passes Senate & Assembly," New York State Senate Press, June 21, 2010, http://www
      .nysenate.gov/press-release/senator-montgomerys-smart-growth-public-infrastructure-
      policy-act-passes-senate-assemb.

16   Jake Cowan with G. Thomas Kingsley, "Using Information in Community Building and Local
      Policy," National Neighborhood Indicators Partnership and The Urban Institute, 3rd ed.,
      June 2007, http://www.urban.org/uploadedpdf/412033_stories_using_information.pdf.

Notes on Contributors

McLain Clutter is an architect and writer who teaches at the University of Michigan Taubman College of Architecture and Urban Planning. His recent essays have appeared in *Grey Room* and *MONU*, and the work of his design practice, MCRD, has been exhibited internationally.

Julia Czerniak is a professor of architecture at Syracuse University and the inaugural director of UPSTATE: A Center for Design, Research, and Real Estate. She is also a registered landscape architect and founder of CLEAR, an interdisciplinary design practice. Czerniak's design work, complemented by a body of writing, focuses on urban landscapes.

Don Mitchell teaches urban, cultural, and Marxist geography at Syracuse University. He is the author of *The Right to the City: Social Justice and the Fight for Public Space* (2003) and, most recently, *They Saved the Crops: Labor Landscape and the Struggle for Industrial Farming in Bracero Era California* (2012).

Edward Mitchell is principal of Edward Mitchell Architects and cofounder of Komanda, an architectural research group. He is an associate professor at the School of Architecture at Yale University, where he teaches theory and design and is director of the post-professional M.Arch. II program.

Hunter Morrison is executive director of the Northeast Ohio Sustainable Communities Consortium, a regional planning coalition. He has been the director of the Center for Urban and Regional Studies and the director of campus planning and community partnerships at Youngstown State University, and has also served as planning director for the city of Cleveland.

Marc Norman is a vice president at Deutsche Bank in its Community Development Finance Group. In this position, he provides loans and investments to organizations serving low-income communities throughout the U.S. With a master's degree in urban planning from

UCLA, Norman has more than fifteen years of experience in the field of affordable housing development and finance.

Mark Robbins is former dean of the Syracuse University School of Architecture and the university's senior advisor for architecture and urban initiatives. He was previously director of design at the National Endowment for the Arts, curator of architecture at the Wexner Center for the Arts, and an associate professor in the Knowlton School of Architecture. He received a fellowship in the visual arts at the Radcliffe Institute and a Rome Prize from the American Academy in Rome. His book *Households* was published by Monacelli Press.

David Grahame Shane is a critic, historian, and adjunct professor of architecture at Columbia University and Cooper Union, both in New York. He has lectured extensively in Europe, the United States, and Asia and published widely in architectural journals. His books include *Recombinant Urbanism: Conceptual Modeling in Architecture, Urban Design and City Theory* (2005) and *Urban Design Since 1945: A Global Perspective* (2011).

Roger Sherman is principal of Roger Sherman Architecture and Urban Design in Los Angeles and codirector of cityLAB, an urban think tank at UCLA. Sherman is the author of several books, including *LA Under the Influence: The Hidden Logic of Urban Property* (2009) and *Re: American Dream: New Housing Prototypes for Los Angeles* (1996), and coeditor of *Fast Forward Urbanism: Rethinking Architecture's Engagement with the City* (2011).

Charles Waldheim is John E. Irving Professor and Chair of the Department of Landscape Architecture at Harvard University's Graduate School of Design. Waldheim coined the term "landscape urbanism" to describe emergent practices at the intersection of contemporary urbanism and landscape. He is a recipient of a Rome Prize fellowship from the American Academy in Rome and has served as the Cullinan Chair at Rice University, a Sanders Fellow at the University of Michigan, and a visiting scholar at the Canadian Centre for Architecture.

Illustration Credits

19, 20 (top): Earth Imaging / Stone / Getty Images

20 (bottom), 24, 42, 44: UPSTATE: Syracuse University School of Architecture ©2012

27, 31, 149–53, 155, 157, 158, 160, 163: Julia Czerniak ©2012

28: Tej Nagaraja / Picture the Homeless ©2011

35: David Heald

37: Jersey City Realty Exchange ©2011

43: Maren Guse ©2010

45: Mark Robbins ©2010

46: Magda Biernat ©2010

51–53, 59, 63, 66: McLain Clutter

55, 56, 58, 60: McLain Clutter, Erica Wannemacher, Bryan Alcorn, and Melinda Rouse

71, 76: Ohio Historical Society

74: Courtesy the Library of Congress

80, 81: Center for Urban and Regional Studies, the City of Youngstown

91, 97: Picture the Homeless ©2011

107, 112, 113: Roger Sherman Architecture and Urban Design, with Greg Kochanowski ©2010

114: Roger Sherman Architecture and Urban Design ©2010

115: Roger Sherman ©2010

116–19: cityLAB / Roger Sherman Architecture and Urban Design ©2010

23, 142, 143, 145: Komanda ©2010

130: DLW Rail Road Collection, Syracuse University ©2011

133: Barry Le Va ©1967 / Courtesy of Daniel Weinberg Gallery

137: Gerhard Richter ©2012

140, 141: Vita Nuova and EMA ©2010

162: The Heidelberg Project Archives / Geronimo Patton and Jennifer Baross

167: Reproduced courtesy of Gregory Crewdson and Gagosian Gallery ©2009

185: Don Fuchs / LOOK / Getty Images

190: Courtesy of S&P / Case-Shiller Home Price Indices March 2011

191: Bill Pugliano / Getty Images News / Getty Images

194, 197: Marc Norman ©2011

196: Google ©2011 and Tele Atlas ©2011

198: Center for Neighborhood Technology ©2003–11